# ATTRACTING
# EQUITY
# INVESTORS

# ENTREPRENEURSHIP AND THE MANAGEMENT OF GROWING ENTERPRISES

## A Sage Publication Series

THE ENTREPRENEURSHIP AND THE MANAGEMENT OF GROWING ENTERPRISES series focuses on leading edge and specialized ideas important to the creation and effective management of new businesses. Each volume provides in-depth, accessible, up-to-date information to graduate and advanced undergraduates students, investors, and entrepreneurs.

SERIES EDITOR  Jerome A. Katz
*Saint Louis University*
*Jefferson Smurfit Center for Entrepreneurial Studies*

ADVISORY BOARD  D. Ray Bagby, *Baylor University*
Donald F. Kuratko, *Ball State University*
Justin Longnecker, *Baylor University*
Ian C. MacMillan, *University of Pennsylvania*
Howard H. Stevenson, *Harvard University*
Frederick C. Scherr, *West Virginia University*
Jeffry A. Timmons, *Babson College*

### BOOKS IN THIS SERIES

*FIELD CASEWORK:*
*Methods for Consulting to Small and Startup Businesses*
Lisa K. Gundry and Aaron A. Buchko

*NEW VENTURE STRATEGY:*
*Timing, Environmental Uncertainty, and Performance*
Dean A. Shepherd and Mark Shanley

*ATTRACTING EQUITY INVESTORS:*
*Positioning, Preparing, and Presenting the Business Plan*
Dean A. Shepherd and Evan J. Douglas

# ATTRACTING EQUITY INVESTORS

## Positioning, Preparing, and Presenting the Business Plan

DEAN A. SHEPHERD
EVAN J. DOUGLAS

SAGE Publications
*International Educational and Professional Publisher*
Thousand Oaks   London   New Delhi

*For information:*

SAGE Publications, Inc.
2455 Teller Road
Thousand Oaks, California 91320
E-mail: order@sagepub.com

SAGE Publications Ltd.
6 Bonhill Street
London EC2A 4PU
United Kingdom

SAGE Publications India Pvt. Ltd.
M-32 Market
Greater Kailash I
New Delhi 110048 India

Printed in the United States of America

**Library of Congress Cataloging-in-Publication Data**

Shepard, Dean A.
  Attracting equity investors: Positioning, preparing, and
presenting the business plan / Dean A. Shepherd,  Evan J. Douglas.
    p. cm. — (Entrepeneurship and the management of growing
enterprises)
  Includes bibliographical references and index.
  ISBN 0-7619-1476-5 (cloth)
  ISBN 0-7619-1477-3 (pbk.)
    1. Business planning. I. Douglas, Evan J., 1946-   II. Title. III.
Series.
  HD30.28 .D685 1998
  658.4'012—ddc21                                98-19760


99  00  01  02  03  04  8  7  6  5  4  3  2  1


| | |
|---|---|
| *Acquiring Editor:* | Marquita Flemming |
| *Editorial Assistant:* | MaryAnn Vail |
| *Production Editor:* | Diana E. Axelsen |
| *Editorial Assistant:* | Nevair Kabakian |
| *Typesetter/Designer:* | Danielle Dillahunt |
| *Cover Designer:* | Candice Harman |

# Contents

List of Tables and Figures     xi

Acknowledgments     xiii

Introduction     xv
  The Purpose of This Book     xv
  What Is Different About This Book?     xvi
  Overview of This Book     xvi
  Note     xviii

1. Sources of Early-Stage Financing     1
  Debt Versus Equity     2
  Categories of Early-Stage Financing     3
  Sources of Early-Stage Funding     3
  Self-Funding With the Help of Family and Friends     4
  Venture Capitalists     5
    *What Else Can Venture Capitalists Offer?*     7
    *The Special Preferences of Venture Capitalists*     7
    *How to Approach a Venture Capitalist*     8
    *Keeping Your Options Open*     8
  Business Angels     9
    *The Preferences of Business Angels*     12
    *How to Contact Business Angels*     12
  Conclusion     14
  Notes     15

2. Roles and Equity Shares in the New Venture     18
  Entrepreneurial Roles     19

The Holder of the Strategic Assets                                    19
The Manager                                                          19
The Investor                                                         20
The Basis for Equity Allocation in a New Business                   20
Conflicts Arising From the Allocation of Equity                     20
The Inventor                                                         22
The Business Planner                                                 23
The Management Team                                                  24
The Investor                                                         26
Recommendations on Equity Allocation                                27
Draw Up an Ownership Plan                                           28
Sequential Allocation of Sweat Equity                               31
Develop an Explicit Protocol for Financial Calls                    32
Establish the Criteria for External Investors                       33
Incentive Contracting With Other Stakeholders                       34
Let the Market Work for You                                         35
Agree on the Investor's Involvement in the Business                 35
Consult an Attorney                                                 36
Conclusion                                                          37
Notes                                                               38

3. Evaluate the Business From the Investor's Perspective            40

What Are Investors Looking For?                                     41
New Ventures Within the Investor's Domain                          41
New Ventures That Provide Superior Value                            42
New Ventures That Serve a Long-Felt Need                            44
A "Proprietary" Position                                            44
Follow-Up Products                                                 46
Points on the Scoreboard                                           46
The Liability of Newness                                            47
Novelty to the Customer                                            47
Novelty to the Producer                                            50
Novelty to Management                                              51
The Impact of Risk Reduction Strategies on
    Consumer Ignorance                                             51
The Impact of Risk Reduction Strategies on
    Producer Ignorance                                             53
Conclusion                                                         54
Notes                                                              55

4. Evaluate the Managers From the Investor's Perspective           57
The Quality of the Management Team                                 58

| | |
|---|---|
| *Diverse and Complementary Skills* | 58 |
| *Relevant Experience* | 61 |
| *Hurt Money* | 62 |
| *The Principal-Agent Problem* | 62 |
| *Boards of Directors* | 63 |
| *Advisory Groups* | 64 |
| Novelty to Management | 64 |
| *The Impact of Risk Reduction Strategies on* | |
| *Novelty to Management* | 67 |
| Conclusion | 68 |
| Notes | 69 |
| 5. The Three-Stage Communication Strategy | 70 |
| *A Strategic Approach to Achieve Your Objective* | 71 |
| How to Get There: The Three-Stage | |
| Communication Approach | 73 |
| *The Purpose of Each Stage* | 73 |
| *Stage I—The Business Plan* | 74 |
| *Stage II—The Presentation* | 74 |
| *Stage III—The Question-and-Answer Period* | 75 |
| *Brevity and Parsimony* | 76 |
| *The Logical Flow of Ideas* | 77 |
| *Building and Maintaining Investor Interest* | 77 |
| *Target the Intended Audience* | 78 |
| Conclusion | 78 |
| 6. Write a Compelling Business Plan | 80 |
| *The Virtues of Parsimony and Persistence* | 81 |
| *Persistence—Keep Revising Until You Run Out of Time* | 81 |
| *Critical Review by an Outside Party* | 82 |
| *The Use of Visual Aids in the Business Plan* | 83 |
| Content and Structure of the Business Plan | 84 |
| *The Executive Summary* | 85 |
| *Company Description* | 89 |
| *What Business Is the New Venture In?* | 89 |
| *The New Product or Service Concept* | 90 |
| *Window of Opportunity and Distinctive Competence* | 91 |
| Market Environment and Competitor Analysis | 94 |
| *Industry Attractiveness* | 95 |
| *Overall Market and Target Segment(s)* | 95 |
| *Competitive Positioning* | 98 |
| *Customers' Decision-Making Process* | 99 |

*Marketing Mix*     100
*Growth Strategy*     102
Research and Development     103
Manufacturing and Operations     105
Organizational Structure, Management, and Ownership     106
    *Organizational Structure*     106
    *Quality of the Management Team*     107
    *Complementarity of the Management Team*     107
    *Ownership Structure*     107
Risk Recognition and Risk Reduction Strategies     108
Financial Details     108
    *Sensitivity and Scenario Analysis*     110
    *Financial Details*     111
The Deal—The Ask and the Offer     112
What Should Go in the Appendixes?     112
Conclusion     113
Notes     113

7. Successfully Presenting and Defending Your Business Plan     114
What Should Be Presented?     115
The Presentation Team     116
    *Dress and Demeanor*     116
    *Who Should Participate?*     118
A Suggested Plan for the Presentation     118
    *Who Should Do the Talking?*     119
Get the Investor Excited About Your Product
    or Service Concept     120
    *Multimedia Presentation*     121
Convince the Investor That the Management
    Team Adds Value     124
Communicate the Financial Viability of the New Venture     125
Pitch the Deal and Begin the Negotiation Process     126
The Q&A Session     127
    *Answer the Question Asked*     127
    *Treat All Questions With Respect*     128
    *Brevity Is a Virtue*     128
    *Responsibility for Particular Questions*     129
    *Let the Leader Lead*     130
    *Don't "Add On" to a Team Member's Answer*     130
Common Questions You May Be Asked     131

Questions on Proprietary Intellectual Property
    *and Its Protection*     132
*Questions on Your Market, Target Customer,*
    *and Market Research*     133
*Questions on Your Marketing Strategy*     133
*Questions on Your Sustainable Competitive Advantages*     134
*Questions on Your Financial Projections*     134
*Questions on the Deal*     134
Conclusion     134
Note     135

8. Valuing the Business and Negotiating the Deal     136
The Valuation of the Business     137
    *Net Present Value Analysis*     138
    *The Internal Rate of Return Method*     141
    *"I Want X Times My Money Back in Y Years."*     142
Assumptions Underlying the Valuation     143
    *Revenue Projections*     143
    *Cost Assumptions*     144
    *Accounting Conventions*     145
    *Time Horizon Selected*     146
    *The Price/Earnings Ratio Selected*     146
Reconciling the Assumptions and Negotiating the Deal     148
    *The Negotiation Process*     148
Creative Financing     150
    *Funding in Stages as Needed*     150
    *Debt Versus Equity*     151
    *Voting Versus Nonvoting Stock*     151
    *Management Contracts and Performance Criteria*     151
    *Taking Options on Management's Share of Equity*     152
    *Sliding Scale Agreements for Management's Share*     153
Conclusion     153
Notes     154

9. Summary and Conclusions     155
Sources of Early-Stage Venture Capital     156
Roles and Equity Shares in the New Venture     157
Evaluate the Business Concept From the
    Investor's Perspective     158
Evaluate the Management Team From the
    Investor's Perspective     159

The Three-Stage Communication Strategy      160
Write a Compelling Business Plan      161
Successfully Presenting and Defending
     Your Business Plan      163
Valuing the Business and Negotiating the Deal      164
Conclusion      164

Index      166

About the Authors      173

# List of Tables and Figures

Table 1.1.  Categories of Early-Stage Financing     3

Table 1.2.  Primary Sources of Early-Stage Funding     3

Table 1.3.  Considerations in Selecting Venture Capitalists     9

Table 1.4.  Profile of the Typical Business Angel     10

Table 2.1.  Reasons for Allocating Equity in Your Business     21

Table 2.2.  The Ownership Plan     29

Table 2.3.  Sequential Allocation of Sweat Equity to Managers     31

Table 6.1.  A "Page Budget" for Your Business Plan     84

Table 6.2.  Risk Recognition and Risk Reduction Strategies for Oceanic Products     109

Table 6.3.  Assumptions Underlying the Scenarios for Oceanic Products     110

Table 7.1.  Suggested Outline and Time Budget for the Presentation     120

Table 7.2.  Suggested Layout for a PowerPoint Slide     123

Figure 7.1 Sample Graph of Financial Performance     126

Table 8.1.  NPV Calculations to Evaluate the New Venture     141

Table 8.2.  RRR Implied by Various Investment Multiples                    142

Table 8.3.  Share of Equity Required to Achieve Several
            RRRs Under Different P/E Ratios                                147

Table 9.1.  Checklist—Sources of Early-Stage Financing                    157

Table 9.2.  Checklist—Roles and Equity Shares in the
            New Venture                                                    159

Table 9.3.  Checklist—Evaluate the Business From the
            Investor's Viewpoint                                           160

Table 9.4.  Checklist—Evaluate the Management Team
            From the Investor's Perspective                               161

Table 9.5.  Checklist—Devising Your Three-Stage
            Communication Strategy                                        162

Table 9.6.  Checklist—Write a Compelling Business Plan                    162

Table 9.7.  Checklist—Successfully Presenting and
            Defending Your Business Plan                                   164

Table 9.8.  Checklist—Valuing the Business and
            Negotiating the Deal                                          165

# Acknowledgments

We wish to acknowledge past Bond University MOOT CORP teams, in particular, Andrew Maxwell, Prue Kellahan, and Kim Goriss (Ecoclear); Richard Sachs, Nicole Martin, David Johnston, and Michael Levens (Decklock); Robert Brough, Tim Zwemer, and Peter Homan (Breeze Technology); and Ed Gordon and Mark Speding (Commercial Marine Products).

Thanks.

*Dean A. Shepherd dedicates this book to his best mates:*
*Susie Leggett, Justin Parer, Brent and Kerrie Shepherd.*

*Evan J. Douglas dedicates this book to his family:*
*Shelly, Andrew, and Meghan.*

# Introduction

## THE PURPOSE OF THIS BOOK

This book is designed to help entrepreneurs gain funding for the launch and/or expansion of their new business venture. It recognizes that the supply of funding for new ventures is scarce, relative to the need for funding from millions of would-be entrepreneurs. Thus, there is very real competition for the funds that are available. The entrepreneur must "stand out" in such competition to obtain funding. He or she must tell a very compelling story in a very convincing manner and be able to answer confidently all questions posed by the potential investor. But more than simply obtaining the funding, the entrepreneur's objective should be to obtain the funding on the best terms possible.

In any market, if the seller provides exactly what the buyer wants and better serves the buyer's needs while pricing competitively, gaining the sale should be a straightforward matter. The same goes for selling part of your business to an investor. You need to understand what the investor is looking for in an investment, qualitatively and quantitatively, and offer that investor a large enough share in the business such that he or she perceives that the investment opportunity is personally interesting, not excessively risky, and sufficiently lucrative.

No venture capitalist will support a business or a management team unless he or she believes in the viability of the business and the competence of the management team. Thus, this book is about organizing your business and then writing and presenting a business plan to convince the investor that the business is a desirable and sufficiently lucrative investment and that the management team is the right group of people to be taking that business opportunity forward toward fruition.

## WHAT IS DIFFERENT ABOUT THIS BOOK?

There are dozens of books available on "how to write a business plan," so why buy this one? Those other books, and there are many good ones,[1] focus on the mechanics of the business plan. That is, they are primarily concerned with the structure and content of the business plan, such as what items or elements should be in it, what the best order of presentation of these elements should be, what market research results should be provided, and so on. We address such concerns in Chapter 6.

This book is about the broader issue of how to raise equity capital for a new business venture. It is more concerned with issues prior to and following the submission of the business plan to a prospective investor than with the actual business plan itself. This book is designed to help the entrepreneur clear the hurdles to obtaining funding (only one of which is the absence of a good business plan). In a nutshell, this book is about making your new venture "investor ready" so that an investor will be attracted to your business and be willing to invest in it now, with minimal changes or disruptions necessary before such investment takes place.

## OVERVIEW OF THIS BOOK

In Chapter 1, we discuss the sources of funding for new ventures. After a brief discussion of the disadvantages of debt funding, we examine the three main sources of equity funding—personal contacts, venture capitalists, and business angels. Strategies for identifying and approaching these sources are outlined and discussed.

Chapter 2 addresses the importance of "getting the house in order" in terms of equity allocation and other agreements among the existing owners and managers, before any investor is approached with an offer of an equity share and a financing role in the business. The importance of specifying roles and performance expectations of all parties is stressed.

The concept of an "ownership plan" is introduced, and a variety of related recommendations follow.

Chapter 3 asks the entrepreneur to view the business through the critical eyes of the investor and consider changes in the business that will make it more attractive to potential investors, before submitting the business plan. Investors have strong preferences for the type of project they will invest in, and the entrepreneur should seek to identify and understand these preferences, select the target investors appropriately, and pitch the business plan and presentation accordingly.

Chapter 4 encourages the entrepreneur to look at him- or herself, and the management team, the way an investor would. That is, the entrepreneur should carefully scrutinize the management team from the investor's viewpoint and be prepared to make changes to themselves, the management team, or both before submitting the business plan.

In Chapter 5, we discuss the business plan as stage I of a three-part communication process that will take place between the entrepreneur and an interested investor. Stage I is the business plan itself, stage II is the presentation, and stage III is the question-and-answer (Q&A) session. The entrepreneur should strategically consider which issues should be presented in the business plan, which in the presentation, and which should be left for the Q&A session.

In Chapter 6, we discuss the first stage of the communication process, which is the business plan. We discuss what should and should not be in the business plan, and how the plan should be structured and written. Suggested topics and space budgets for each of these are provided. Examples from other business plans are shown to illustrate the power of careful word choice and idea sequencing.

In Chapter 7, we consider the second and third stages of the communication process with a potential investor, namely, the presentation and the Q&A session. Based on our experience, we provide a number of hints and suggestions for the structuring of the presentation and the conduct of these sessions, to help the investor learn what he or she needs to know to be comfortable about investing in your business.

Chapter 8 is concerned with valuing the business properly and negotiating an appropriate share of the equity in exchange for the funding received. If the entrepreneur fully understands the basis on which the investor will want to value the business, he or she will be prepared for the negotiation session that will take place if the investor is interested in buying equity in the business.

Chapter 9 presents a summary of the most important issues and provides a checklist for the entrepreneur to consider before submitting the business plan to an interested investor.

So, what are you waiting for? Life is short, and there is much to be achieved. Read on!

## NOTE

1. See, for example, the following:

Arkebauer, J. B. (1995). *The McGraw-Hill guide to writing a high-impact business plan. A proven blueprint for entrepreneurs.* New York: McGraw-Hill.

Bangs, D. H. (1995). *The business planning guide. Creating a plan for success in your own business* (7th ed.). Chicago, IL: Upstart.

DeThomas, A., & Fredenberger, W. B. (1995). *Writing a convincing business plan.* Hauppage, NY: Barron's.

Kars, K. (Ed.). (1995). *Business plans handbook.* New York: Gale Research, Inc.

For more such books and a brief synopsis of some of them, see Ryans, C. C. (1997). Resources. *Journal of Small Business Management, 35*(2), 95-98.

# 1 | Sources of Early-Stage Financing

The number of new enterprises launched in the United States has grown rapidly from about 1 million in 1981 to 18 million in 1988, and it is estimated to reach 30 million by the year 2000.[1] These new,[2] small, and expanding firms generate virtually all new jobs.[3] They also generate 50% of all innovations and 95% of all radical innovations.[4] Access to early-stage capital is one of the key contributing factors to new venture survival and growth and, thus, to increased employment and ongoing technological innovation.

Raising capital is important to all firms but in particular to new ventures whose growth gives them an amazing appetite for cash. For example, Briazz, a Seattle-based salad and sandwich café chain, required equity capital to fund national expansion. They raised $19 million from a group of investors. The iCat.Corp required and obtained a similar amount of money to maintain their lead in creating software for interactive internet catalogues.[5] Growing companies like Briazz and iCat.Corp may require a number of infusions of cash to fund their continued growth. On the other hand, Chris, a retired supermarket manager who intends to set up Sail Away, a yacht-charter business on Grand Cayman island in the Caribbean, expects to require only initial funding, inasmuch as operating revenues are expected to exceed operating expenses once he begins operations.

Thus, some companies require only an initial infusion of cash and can fund future growth from profits (retained earnings), whereas other

1

potential business owners are not seeking growth and seek only the capital necessary to start or purchase the business.

## DEBT VERSUS EQUITY

The two main sources of capital are debt and equity. Debt usually is more difficult to obtain, because new ventures lack a track record of sales and usually also lack collateral to pledge against the loan. Debt also places a strain on the cash flow of the new venture, as it requires regular cash payments regardless of performance.

The iCat.Corp probably had difficulty obtaining a loan because the company's greatest assets are the skills, knowledge, and experience of their programmers; bankers typically are unwilling to consider such intangible assets as collateral for the loan. Whereas Sail Away may be able to use the yacht as collateral to obtain a loan, there may not be sufficient clients in the early years to provide the necessary revenue to meet the loan repayments. Because raising debt is so difficult for most new ventures, this book concentrates on helping new ventures raise equity capital. Equity capital involves giving away some ownership of the company in return for funds, that is, an investor is buying into your company. Using equity rather than debt offers advantages and disadvantages to the business owner.

To obtain the necessary funds the owners of Briazz, iCat.Corp, and Sail Away would have given up some of their ownership in the company. For example, the founders of a research company offered an investor (with experience in the particular research industry) 40% ownership in the business for $400,000. Previously, the five founders each owned 20% of the business and had rights to 100% of any profits, but after the infusion of funds they each now own 12% of the business and must share profits. (It should be noted that the wealth of the business has just increased by $400,000 and the probability of generating profits also has increased.) Whereas the founders now must share future profits (if they materialize), they also are sharing the risk. Equity financing does not require a regular payment to the investor, as does debt financing, which has the important effect of reducing pressures on cash flow. Reduced pressure on cash flow is particularly important for new ventures in their early stages of development.

## CATEGORIES OF EARLY-STAGE FINANCING

The early stages of financing are summarized in Table 1.1[6]

TABLE 1.1. Categories of Early-Stage Financing

---

**Seed financing** Typically refers to investment in proving a concept to qualify for start-up capital. This could involve the building and testing of prototypes, researching and writing a business plan, including market research, and the bringing together of a management team. We include within this category research and development tax-advantaged partnerships. The capital involved at the seed stage typically is small relative to the other stages, although it represents the highest degree of risk.

**Start-Up financing** Prelaunch funding for ventures to finance initial marketing research and prototype development of their product or service to the stage of commercial readiness and to perform prelaunch marketing activities.

**First-Stage financing** Provides the venture with funds to begin full-scale production operations and marketing and sales activities.

**Development financing** Provides funding for a business that has an established track record of early sales but that needs cash to keep growing.

---

## SOURCES OF EARLY-STAGE FUNDING

The main sources of funds invested in new ventures are shown in Table 1.2.

TABLE 1.2. Primary Sources of Early-Stage Funding

---

**Personal sources** These funds are what the entrepreneur can raise from his or her personal assets and from family and friends who are linked to the entrepreneur emotionally, by blood ties, or both.

**Venture capitalists** These are professional, institutional investors who take equity positions in new high-risk, high-return private firms.

**Business angels** Also known as informal investors, these are typically high-net-worth individuals (excluding the entrepreneur and his or her family and friends) who invest their funds in high-risk, high-return private companies.

**Employees** Employees who get in on the ground floor may contribute funds or alternatively accept a lower-than-market-value salary in exchange for stock in the business.

**Customers** Customers may agree to deposits (or payment in full) before production takes place and so ease the new venture's need for operating capital.

**Suppliers** Suppliers may agree to defer payment for components and raw materials and so ease the new venture's cash flow problem.

---

In this chapter, we are mainly concerned with the first three sources of new venture funding, inasmuch as these represent the major sources of funds for new ventures whereas the latter three sources are usually only minor sources of funding, if they are possible at all.

## SELF-FUNDING WITH THE HELP
## OF FAMILY AND FRIENDS

According to the Small Business Administration (SBA), about 95% of all start-ups are financed entirely through a patchwork of personal assets, personal loans, and money from relatives and friends. This is often called "bootstrapping," in reference to lifting oneself off the ground by one's own bootstraps (which is very hard to do!). This is the most common source of early-stage funding, because the capital required is usually relatively small, with the promise of great things ahead. It is often difficult for family and friends to say no to the request for funds, as they want to be supportive of their friend or family member and will be reluctant to let any reservations they have about the business concept stop them from helping.

---

For example, Chris Stuart and Michael Michalski used their termination from Laser Artistry Inc. as the trigger to start their own business, Laser Force. Laser Force's primary product and service is laser display entertainment for corporate theater, festivals, and special events. The two entrepreneurs learned quickly that banks were unwilling to lend them money to purchase the equipment they required to make this business a success. They turned to and found support from family and friends. The $80,000 from family and friends, in conjunction with a grant of $6,000 from the Milwaukee Department of City Development, was sufficient for them to pursue their dream.[7]

---

Often the family or loved ones who are asked to invest lack sufficient business expertise to evaluate the investment, and they tend to underestimate the risk.[8] Because they trust the person requesting the funds, they invest primarily on that basis, with little consideration for business viability. This is the major reason why the cost of this capital is inexpensive relative to the business risk.

The family or friend investor often brings little of positive value to the business relationship beyond the money. Conversely, the family or friend investor brings an added emotional risk for the entrepreneur. If the business fails, then both parties stand to lose more than just the business and their money. Typically, the entrepreneur needs to have family and friends who can act as a sanctuary, where the entrepreneur can escape from the pressures of business. But when these people are part owners, they are enthusiastically interested in how "their" business is going, which makes it difficult to separate business from family or social activities. Chapter 3, which concerns the understanding between initial investors and members of the entrepreneurial team, is especially important when family and friends also are investors.

## VENTURE CAPITALISTS

There are more than 500 venture capital firms in the United States, which in aggregate manage approximately $35 billion invested in new ventures, with available capital currently reported to exceed $15 billion. In 1995, according to the company Boston Economics, venture capital firms invested $3.86 billion in 1,128 ventures.[9] Nevertheless, the amount invested by venture capital firms could be higher, according to the National Venture Capital Association, which reported that more than $10 billion was invested in 1,502 deals in 1996.[10] The typical investment of a small venture capital firm is between $500,000 and $1.5 million, with the larger megafunds investing up to $100 million and not less than $1 million or $2 million.[11] Venture capital firms typically are not interested in the "small stuff" below half a million.

The investment managers of the venture capital funds are the people we refer to as *venture capitalists*. They receive their rewards through salaries and management fees and through bonuses when capital gains are realized. Whether earning quick capital gains is their motivation or not, venture capitalists are particularly interested in (some are *only* interested in) those ventures that can go public in 3 to 5 years. Initial public offerings (IPOs) provide the perfect vehicle for the venture capitalist to exit with high returns. Neil Rodberg, Director of Operations at MIT's Business Angel Network, reported that venture capitalists expect a 35% to 40% return compounded annually, prefer to concentrate on the second and middle stages of venture development, and rarely fund ventures seeking less than $2 million.[12]

Venture capitalists prefer to co-invest with other venture capital firms rather than invest alone. Seventy percent of venture-capital-backed firms in low-technology businesses had more than one venture capitalist involved, and this figure rises to 86% for high-innovation businesses.[13] Co-investing typically is used by venture capitalists to decrease their risk exposure in any one venture. More recently, venture capitalists have leaned more toward investing in information technology, which now accounts for 58% of the overall venture capital raised.[14]

Venture capitalists have considerable power, and you can expect them to wield it. The source of that power derives from the fact that they control the funds and can demand seats on the board of directors. Whereas they typically do not seek a majority share of the ownership, they do expect management to perform. This is often done through a series of tight targets or milestones that must be met. If management fails to meet these milestones, the venture capitalist can be instrumental in the removal of a CEO. In fact, replacement of the CEO is quite common among venture-capital-backed firms, with 40% of high-performing companies and 74% of poor-performing companies having their CEOs changed at least once, according to one study.[15]

It is often reported that a venture-capital-backed company has a greater chance of survival.[16] This is because venture capitalists use their expertise to select winners and do not invest in those they perceive to be doomed to failure. Their understanding of what it takes to succeed, and their perception of "red flags" that do not auger well for success, allow venture capitalists to make suggestions (or set conditions if they are to invest), which add value to the venture by improving its chances of success. Some venture capitalists are more active in their investments than others. The more active venture capitalists spend 35 hours per month per venture assisting the management team primarily in strategic matters, whereas less active firms spend less than 7 hours per month per investment.[17]

## WHAT ELSE CAN VENTURE CAPITALISTS OFFER?

Venture capitalists can bring much more to the new venture, in addition to the money. One of the most important benefits arising from a relationship with a venture capitalist is access to his or her extensive network. This is often used to find and recruit top quality management, to find other co-investors for immediate or follow-up investment, to introduce the venture to important service providers, such as specialized accountants, and to help find and develop necessary strategic alliances.

Venture capitalists also serve in a role as sounding board for management ideas and are a valuable source of strategic and operational advice. Being backed by a venture capital company provides legitimacy even outside the venture capitalist's network. It may provide customers confidence to purchase from the venture knowing that it is venture capital backed and unlikely to disappear overnight.

## THE SPECIAL PREFERENCES OF VENTURE CAPITALISTS

Venture capitalists differ in the initial criteria they use to select those new ventures they will consider for investment. These criteria include type of industry, industry stage of development, geographic location, size of investment required, and other items. These are detailed in lists of venture capitalists, for example *Pratt's Venture Capital Guide.*[18] The new entrepreneur must search through the list of venture capitalists to find those whose selection criteria best fit their venture. This list needs to be further reduced to about 10 venture capitalists who appear to have the best fit with the company, on the basis of their criteria and their ability to satisfy the requirements of the venture. The venture capitalists chosen should be ones who typically take the lead investment: They will be able to attract additional investment from so-called passive venture capitalists, if necessary. Approaching more than 10 venture capitalists may give the impression to any particular venture capitalist that the venture is "overshopped."

## HOW TO APPROACH A VENTURE CAPITALIST

The best first contact with a venture capitalist is through a referral, preferably from an accountant, a banker, a fellow entrepreneur, or someone who the venture capitalist trusts and respects. That person would make a phone call to the venture capitalist and suggest that the venture capitalist review your business plan. This contact with the venture capitalist's network is not always available.

Contact with venture capitalists sometimes can be made through venture capital forums. For example, the annual Florida Venture Capital Conference attempts to match entrepreneurs with venture capitalists. Reviewers narrow down 80 to 100 applications to 25 businesses that earn the right to make a 12-minute presentation of their business to the venture capitalist delegates.[19] If you were able to have a positive impact on one or more of the venture capitalists, they would contact you to request a business plan and, it is hoped, a meeting. Venture capital forums are held in many cities in the United States and often are reported in the local newspapers.

## KEEPING YOUR OPTIONS OPEN

As negotiations with one venture capitalist begin, and even as they progress in what might seem like a long way down the track, it is advisable to keep other avenues open, in case these negotiations fail. Venture capitalists often can spend considerable time assessing and discussing your venture, which may signal that a deal is imminent, only to withdraw at a later stage for a variety of reasons, not all of which relate to the nature of the new venture. Even if negotiations proceed to a satisfactory conclusion, if you have left yourself with no alternative source of funds your bargaining power and/or confidence to negotiate for specific points could be significantly diminished.

Whereas the investor is performing "due diligence" on you, you should be simultaneously performing due diligence on the investor. Make sure he or she or they can add value to your company over and above the money. Part of this is making sure you have a good feeling about them. Ask yourself whether you could work with these people, because in essence you are entering into a partnership with them. They

TABLE 1.3. Considerations in Selecting Venture Capitalists

---

1. Do they invest in your type of business (e.g., industry, stage of development, geography, and so forth)?
2. How extensive and useful is their network?
3. Are they an effective sounding board and source of advice and support?
4. Does the wider community respect them?
5. Do they add value to the business over and above the infusion of capital?
6. Is there a personality "fit" between the venture capitalists and members of your management team?

---

must be the right venture capitalist for you, just as you must be a venture and management team with which they can feel comfortable. Table 1.3 displays the key criteria an entrepreneur should consider before selecting a venture capital firm.

How do we gain information about venture capitalists to answer these important questions? You can obtain considerable insight into these issues from a venture capital firm's brochure or other sources, such as the business press, by looking at the type of investments they have made and their success with those investments. Many venture capital firms also have web pages that provide considerable information, for example, www.Ent.com, www.TA.com, www.Accel.com, and www.Canaan.com.

In the brochures or on the web pages, the venture capital firms may list present or past firms in which they have invested. Request permission from the venture capital firm to contact the owner or manager of investee firms with the purpose of evaluating the venture capitalist. The venture capital firm is likely to be impressed with the professionalism of conducting your own due diligence into potential investors. In the unlikely situation that the venture capital firm tries to dissuade you from contacting its investee firms, this should provide a warning signal that this venture capital firm might not be the one for you.

## BUSINESS ANGELS

Business angels, also known as informal investors, represent the largest (dollar value) source of equity funds, although the exact amount is difficult to determine because of the privacy of most arrangements. It

TABLE 1.4.  Profile of the Typical Business Angel

| Variable | Typical Business Angel |
| --- | --- |
| Age | 47-54 years |
| Sex | Male |
| Annual family income | $80,000 to $100,000 |
| Net worth | $1 million |
| Experience | Extensive experience and some entrepreneurial in nature |
| Education | Typically at least a Bachelor's degree and more than half with advanced degrees |
| Number of investments | Two investments every 3 years |
| Investment rate | Invest in 8% of opportunities identified |
| Average amount invested | $59,000 |
| Preferred stage | Start-up (56%) and infant or young firms (24%) |
| Co-investment | Invest alone |
| Control | 56% maintain a minority voting position |

has been estimated that the portfolio of invested funds by business angels in 1987 was about $50 billion,[20] with approximately $32.7 billion representing equity funds invested.[21] This capital, introduced by business angels, financed in excess of 20,000 businesses in the United States (and these estimates are more than 10 years old). Clearly, business angels are an important source of funds.

On the basis of studies in Canada, Sweden, the United Kingdom, and the United States, the typical profile of a business angel is somewhat similar[22] and is represented in Table 1.4.

One of the most significant and interesting aspects of business angels' investment behavior is their emphasis on early-stage ventures.[23] Obermayer proposed that there is an "equity financing gap" between those ventures that are seen to be too small, too illiquid, and/or too risky for venture capitalists but require too many resources to be supplied by the entrepreneur, their family, friends, or both.[24] Whereas there is considerable overlap between the different sources of capital, business angles are the most important source of funds that fill this "equity financing gap."

Business angels typically have started their own business or have experience managing a new venture. Mr. Kanwal Rekhi, a business angel, believes that business angels are not as stringent as venture capitalists in terms of due diligence, preferring to rely on qualitative assessment and past experiences to evaluate a project idea[25] (i.e., business angels often rely on their gut reactions). They hope to be able to use this experience to help the venture in which they invest improve its performance. Therefore, business angels typically take an active role in the venture. By *active*, we mean being a director of the company, consulting with the CEO, or both. In the United States, business angels are actively involved in the venture 4 hours a week, on average, for the first 6 months and 3.5 hours per week thereafter[26] and 1 to 2 days a week for UK business angels.[27]

---

*Example*: Mr. Rangaswami could be considered a typical business angel. He is a 42-year-old former vice president of worldwide marketing of Baan Co., a Dutch software maker. He was able to exercise his share options in Baan and exit the company a wealthy man. Since leaving Baan in 1995, he has invested $250,000 of his personal funds in a variety of technology companies. He is still searching for companies that will benefit not only from his money but from his practical advice. Bringing more to the relationship than just money, such as the practical advice provided by Mr. Rangaswami, can make a big difference to a new venture's performance.[28]

---

Being able to take an active role is an important (nonfinancial) decision criterion for the business angel (others may include environmental concerns or desire for local economic development). The entrepreneur may be able to benefit from the angel's desire to be involved, in terms of reducing the cost of the finance, not to mention the benefits flowing from the free consultation and access to the knowledge and network base the business angel brings. This issue also has a flip side: The entrepreneur needs to be prepared and open to the business angel's active involvement. As is discussed in Chapter 2, the relationship between the entrepreneur and the investor should be clearly defined and understood by both parties to maximize the benefits and at the same time minimize what might be regarded as meddling.

THE PREFERENCES OF BUSINESS ANGELS

The desire to be active in their investments is one of the reasons that business angels typically invest within a 100-mile radius of where they work and live. Over 70% invest within 50 miles of home. Investing outside this range would decrease their ability to be active and also their ability to monitor their investment. Close proximity of their investment activity is also not surprising when you consider the way that they obtain their deals. Business angels are more aware of opportunities in their local area, and they are highly reliant on their localized referral network to hear about deals. Not only are they reliant on their network to hear about deals but their network acts like a first-stage screening process, inasmuch as network members will not want to introduce fatally flawed business concepts to the business angel.

Business angels also prefer to invest in markets and industries in which they have substantial knowledge, although by some reports they place greater emphasis on investing in familiar people than they do on familiar markets or industries.[29] As they have less opportunity to diversify their business risk, they concentrate on ensuring that the entrepreneur holds similar interests to themselves and that they can monitor progress based on their personal knowledge and involvement. They are usually prepared to take a relatively long-term view of the investment.[30]

HOW TO CONTACT BUSINESS ANGELS

This introduces one of the biggest problems with raising equity funding from business angels—they are invisible to most people. Investing in new ventures is not their full-time job and thus they tend to be somewhat ad hoc in their pursuit of investments. They are a diverse group of people who guard their privacy and anonymity fiercely (as you would if people were always asking you for money!). The best way to contact business angels is to use your own network and hope that the business angel's network and your network overlap somewhere. Therefore, you must "milk" your network to search for and obtain a meeting with a business angel. Look toward acquaintances who own their own business as a possible source of referral. The opportunity to increase the number of such acquaintances is through groups, such as the local chamber of commerce, alumni associations, or social clubs (e.g., Rotary, Lions, etc.).

From Table 1.4, presented earlier, we know that business angels are wealthy individuals. Wealthy individuals usually have strong relationships with their attorneys, accountants, and bankers. Ask your attorney, accountant, and/or banker (if you have one) for any possible leads. Whereas they may not know a business angel directly, their network extends to others within their profession. It is hoped that this extended network is sufficient to provide a referral to at least one business angel.

You would almost certainly increase your exposure to both business angels and venture capitalists by entering and, it is hoped, winning business plan competitions, inventors' awards, or both. For example, EcoClear, after winning the 1996 International MOOT CORP competition at the University of Texas, was approached by a business angel and an initial meeting was arranged for the following week.

Access to one business angel, even if he or she is not ready to invest in your deal, may in fact be your best contact for finding other business angels. Business angels typically know each other through previous business and funding together. Business angels are 40% more likely to invest in a venture if a close personal colleague referred the deal to them.[31] Fortunately (or unfortunately, if it works against you) serendipity also plays a role in the investments a business angel makes.

To find business angels, you must get a referral and permission to use that person's name when you contact the business angel. Business angels, in effect, use their network as the first step in the screening process. For example, an accountant is unlikely to refer a business to his client (the business angel) if that business does not look like a promising investment. If the accountant continually refers nonviable businesses to the angel, he or she is likely to damage an important relationship. Therefore, business angels look more favorably on businesses that have been referred by someone from within their network, as these businesses have already passed an initial hurdle.

Business angels recently have become more visible through participation in matchmaking services that match investors to potential investees. For example, Colorado Capital Alliance matches angels with entrepreneurs. The nonprofit company is only 1 year old and already has 60 business angels and 130 entrepreneurial firms in its database. It does not receive commission from successful matches but charges entrepreneurs $200 for a 12-month listing.[32] Private Capital Clearinghouse, Inc. (Pri-Cap) is a national market for private capital linking entrepreneurs requiring $5 million or less with business angels using the internet.[33] PriCap charges a $150 membership fee for U.S. companies and a $500 fee for listing the business for a 6-month period. PriCap can be found at *www.pricap.com.*

### Timing

It typically takes about 4 months to obtain a decision and actually receive the money from an informal investor, once they have been found, compared to about 6 months for venture capitalists.[34] Thus, the entrepreneur should not expect any immediate solution to his or her cash flow problem and must instead practice forward planning to identify the need for funding long before that need becomes urgent.

## CONCLUSION

New businesses seeking early-stage funding typically need relatively small amounts of funding to help them get off the ground. This would appear to suit a relationship being formed with a business angel, inasmuch as venture capitalists prefer to invest larger sums (usually more than $1 million), and preferably in later stages, as they don't have as much time to be actively involved. Larger investments decrease the total number of investees per portfolio and thereby decrease the amount of time they need to spend overseeing their investees.

Neil Rodberg, Director of Operations at the MIT Business Angel Network, commented that business angels are more patient and willing to accept lower returns, that is, 20% to 25% compared with venture capitalists' 35% to 40% (compounded annually). It is important to realize that once a deal is in place, the negotiation environment is expected to give way to a commonality of purpose and an environment of support (an *esprit de corps*). The relationship between the entrepreneurial team and investor should be considered a strategic alliance. Steiner believes that staged financing requires a clear understanding of each collaborative role in the enterprise.[35] These roles are discussed further in Chapter 2 and managing the negotiation process is discussed in Chapter 8.

## NOTES

1. Timmons, J. A. (1994). *New venture creation: Entrepreneurship for the 21st century* (4th ed.). Boston, MA: Irwin.

2 Approximately one million new ventures every year.

3. Timmons, J. A. (1994). *New venture creation: Entrepreneurship for the 21st century* (4th ed.) Boston, MA: Irwin.

Vesper, K. H. (1980). *New venture strategies.* Englewood Cliffs, NJ: Prentice Hall.

4. Timmons, J. A. (1994). *New venture creation: Entrepreneurship for the 21st century* (4th ed.). Boston, MA: Irwin.

5. Wilson, W. (1997, November 4). Investors pour $136 million into state companies. *Seattle Post-Intelligencer,* p. 1.

6. Financing well-established businesses for the purposes of expansion, mezzanine, and investor buyouts are not within the scope of this book.

7. Dries, M. (1997, September 12). Beam them up. *The Business Journal, 14*(50), 8.

8. This may not be have been the case with Laser Force.

9. Most of these ventures were founded pre-1995.

10. The reports from Boston Economics and the National Venture Capital Association differ by more than $6 billion. This difference can be attributed to either a one-year difference in reporting, different definitions used, or both. These studies still provide an approximate size of the venture capital industry in the United States.

11. Timmons, J. A. (1994). *New venture creation: Entrepreneurship for the 21st century* (4th ed.). Boston, MA: Irwin.

12. Bylinski, G. (1995). Who will feed the startups? In C. M. Mason, R. T. Harrison, & P. Allen (Eds.), *Informal venture capital: A study of the investment process, the post-investment experience and investment performance* (p. 98). Chicago, IL: Fortune Source Qualifier.

13. Bygrave, W. (1987). Syndicated investments of venture capital firms: Networking perspective. *Journal of Business Venturing, 2*(2), 139-154.

14. Gleba, D. (1996). Traditional VCs face increasing competition. *Upside, 8*(10), 118.

15. Rosenstein, J., Bruno, A., Bygrave, W., & Taylor, N. (1989). Do venture capitalists on boards of portfolio companies add value besides money? In R. H. Brockhaus, Sr., N. C. Churchill, J. A. Katz, B. A. Kirchhoff, K. H. Vespter, & W. E. Wetzel, Jr. (Eds.), *Frontiers of entrepreneurship research* (pp. 216-229). Wellesley, MA: Babson College.

16. Sandberg, W. R., & Hofer, C.W. (1987). Improving new venture performance: The role of strategy, industry structure and the entrepreneur. *Journal of Business Venturing, 2*(1), 5-28.

17. Elango, B., Fried, V. H., Hisrich, R. D., & Polonchek, A. (1995). How venture capital firms differ? *Journal of Business Venturing, 10*(2), 157-179.

18. Pratt, S. E. (1987). Overview and introduction to the venture capital industry. In S. Pratt & J. Morris (Eds.), *Pratt's guide to venture capital sources* (11th ed.). Wellesley, MA: Venture Economics.

19. Lunsford, D. (1997, September 26). Venture forum seeking candidates for capital. *South Florida Business Journal, 18*(6), 4.

20. Wetzel, W. E., Jr. (1987). The informal risk capital market: Aspects of scale and efficiency. In N.C. Churchill, J. Hornaday, B. Kirchhoff, O.Krasner, & K. Vesper (Eds.), *Frontiers of entrepreneurship research* (pp. 412-428). Wellesley, MA: Babson College.

21. Gaston, R. J., & Bell, S. E. (1988). *The informal supply of capital* (Report prepared for the Office of Economic Research, U.S. Small Business Administration). Cleveland, OH: Applied Economics Group.

22. Freear, J., & Wetzel, W. E., Jr. (1992). The informal venture capital market in the 1990s. In D. J. Sexton & J. D. Kasarada (Eds.), *Entrepreneurship in the 1990s*(pp. 462-486). Boston: PWS-Kent.

Gaston, R. J. (1989). *Finding private venture capital for your firm: A complete guide.* New York: John Wiley.

Harrison, R. T., & Mason, C. M. (1992). Informal risk capital in the United Kingdom. In N. C. Churchill, S. Birley, W. D. Bygrave, D. E. Muzyka, C. Wahlbin, & W. E. Wetzel, Jr. (Eds.), *Frontiers of entrepreneurial research* (pp. 388-404). Wellesley, MA: Babson College.

Landstrom, H. (1993). Informal risk capital in Sweden and some international comparisons. *Journal of Business Venturing, 8,* 525-540.

Mason, C. M., & Harrison, R.H. (1994). Informal venture capital in the UK. In A. Hughes & D. J. Storey (Eds.), *Finance and the small firm* (pp. 64-111). London: Routledge.

Mason, C. M., & Harrison, R. H. (1996). Why "business angels" say no: A case study of opportunities rejected by an informal investor syndicate. *International Small Business Journal, 14*(2), 35-51.

Riding, A., Dal Cin, P., Duxbury, L., Haines, G., & Safrata, R. (1993). *Informal investors in Canada: The identification of salient characteristics.* Ottawa: Carleton University.

Venture Economics (1990). *Annual review: Venture capital.* Newark, NJ: Author.

23. Freear, J., & Wetzel, W. E., Jr. (1988). Equity financing for new technology based firms. In B. A. Kirchhoft, W. A. Long, W. E. McMullan, K. H. Vesper, & W. E. Wetzel, Jr. (Eds.), *Frontiers of entrepreneurship research* (pp. 347-367). Wellesley, MA: Babson College.

Freear, J., & Wetzel, W. E., Jr. (1990). Who bankrolls high-tech entrepreneurs? *Journal of Business Venturing, 5*(2), 77-89.

24. Obermayer, J. H. (1983). The capital crunch: Small high technology companies and national objectives during a period of severe debt and equity shortages. *Research and Planning.* Waltham, MA: Bentley College.

25. Sreenivas, I. S. (1997, September 29). "Looking for an investment from above. Have more than your prayers ready when you deal with these angels." *The Business Journal, 15*(22), 33.

26. Neiswander, D. K. (1985). Informal seed stage investors. In J. A. Hornaday, E. B. Shils, J. A. Timmons, & K. H. Vesper (Eds.), *Frontiers of entrepreneurship research* (pp. 142-154). Wellesley, MA: Babson College.

27. Mason, C.M., Harrison, R.T., & Allen, P. (Eds.). (1995). Informal venture capital: A study of the investment process, the post-investment experience and investment performance. Chicago, IL: Fortune Source Qualifier.

28. Mehta, S. N. (1997, August 25). The guardians: New breed of investor brings more than cash to hopeful start-ups—Shunning venture capital, businesses seek "angels" with industry experience—Mr. Rangaswami's options. *Wall Street Journal,* p. A1.

29. Fiet, J. O. (1991). Network reliance by venture capital firms and business angels: An empirical and theoretical test. In N. C. Churchill, W. D. Bygrave, J. G. Covin, D. L. Sexton, D. P.

Slevin, K. H. Vesper, & W. E. Wetzel, Jr. (Eds.), *Frontiers of entrepreneurship research* (pp. 445-455). Wellesley, MA: Babson College.

Kelly, P., & Hay, M. (1996). Serial investors: An exploratory study. In P. D. Reynolds, S. Birley, J. Butler, W. Bygrave, P. Davidsson, W. Gartner, & P. P. McDougall (Eds.), *Frontiers of entrepreneurship research* (pp. 329-343). Wellesley, MA: Babson College.

30. Harrison, R. T., & Mason, C. M. (1996). Developing the informal venture capital market: A review of DTI's informal investment demonstration projects. *Regional Studies, 30,* 765-772.

31. Harr, N. W., Starr, J., & MacMillan, I. C. (1988). Informal risk capital investors: Investment patterns on the East Coast of the U.S.A. *Journal of Business Venturing, 3*(1), 11-29.

32. Svaldi, A. (1997, October 31). Group matches angels with business owners: Colorado Capital Alliance helps business startups find money easily and affordably. *The Denver Business Journal, 49*(8), 5.b.

33. PriCap also links entrepreneurs with "natural allies," such as attorneys, accountants, and universities.

34. Freear, J., Sohl, J. A., & Wetzel, W. E., Jr. (1990). Raising venture capital: Entrepreneurs' views of the process. In N. C. Churchill, W. D. Bygrave, J. A. Hornaday, D. F. Muzyka, K. H. Vesper, & W. E. Wetzel, Jr. (Eds.), *Frontiers of entrepreneurial research* (pp. 223-237). Wellesley, MA: Babson College.

Freear, J., & Wetzel, W. E., Jr. (1992). The informal venture capital market in the 1990s. In D. J. Sexton & J. D. Kasarada (Eds.), *Entrepreneurship in the 1990s* (pp. 462-486). Boston: PWS-Kent.

35. Steiner, L., & Greenwood, R. (1995). Venture capitalist relationships in the deal structuring and post-investment stages of new firm creation. *Journal of Management Studies, 32,* 337-357.

# 2 | Roles and Equity Shares in the New Venture

The creation, development, and management of a new venture is often a team effort, and there are distinct roles for each member of the entrepreneurial team within the new venture. The main roles in an entrepreneurial team are those of the people who own the intellectual property, who manage its commercialization, and who are willing to fund its commercialization.

Although these are treated as three separate roles in this chapter, in many practical cases the same person may wear all three hats, or two of the hats, and so on. But even when the entrepreneur can afford to personally fund the start-up of the business, as do 95% of new businesses, sooner or later he or she will be looking for external funding to support the investment necessary to develop the business if and when the business "takes off."

Notwithstanding the often spectacular case of the solo entrepreneur, and inasmuch as entrepreneurial teams (of specialists) tend to be more successful than solo entrepreneurs (although there are many highly visible exceptions), it is useful to discuss the interaction between the persons who take the main roles in an entrepreneurial team.

## ENTREPRENEURIAL ROLES

### THE HOLDER OF THE STRATEGIC ASSETS

The person who owns or holds the rights to the strategic assets (such as the intellectual property or the assets around which the business will be built) is the foundation of the new business. The intellectual property might be protected by a patent from the United States Patent and Trademark Office and/or from other patent authorities around the world or simply might be trade secrets that are proprietary to this new venture. Alternatively, someone may have thought of a new service concept, and keeping the concept secret for as long as possible may allow the new venture to get a jump-start on imitators. Or someone, such as a franchisee, may have purchased the rights to use the idea from someone who owns the rights. In another case, someone may own a particular asset or property that would form the basis for a new business. Thus, the holder of the strategic assets has control (at least temporarily) over intellectual property, brand names, a service concept, or some other asset that is expected to provide a basis for competitive advantage in an existing or new market.

### THE MANAGER

The manager role typically is performed by an individual or a team of people with business-planning skills, strategic-marketing expertise, and the necessary leadership and management skills to take the often vulnerable new venture through the implementation steps to product launch and beyond. Especially these days, such managers need to have a business school degree, preferably an MBA containing several "entrepreneurship" courses, inasmuch as the competition almost certainly will have such business school training, and nobody should want the business to perish for lack of properly trained management. Even when a reasonably good business plan has been written by the inventor (a relatively rare situation, inasmuch as managers and inventors are typically cut from different cloth) the manager or management team is likely to rewrite the plan to fit with its perception of the environment and the optimal strategy for the venture.

THE INVESTOR

Inventors typically have more good ideas for new businesses, and managers typically have more opportunities to manage new ventures, than they can finance to fruition. The inventor may have dissipated his or her resources in pursuit of patent protection, prototype building, or unsuccessful attempts to market the new product. The manager recently may have completed business school and still is carrying a large burden of student loans necessary to gain a good business education. Hence, he or she will be looking for someone with money to invest in his or her new business venture. The investor is the party who is willing to put capital at risk to fund the establishment of the business and the probable operating deficit of the early days.

## THE BASIS FOR EQUITY ALLOCATION
## IN A NEW BUSINESS

Equity in new ventures typically is awarded for one of seven main reasons, as indicated in Table 2.1. In many cases, the same individual(s) may "earn" equity from more than one of these sources, of course.

## CONFLICTS ARISING FROM
## THE ALLOCATION OF EQUITY

Common causes of friction among parties involved in a new business venture are disputes that arise (perhaps after smoldering beneath the surface) concerning the relative shareholdings of those parties. Perhaps the inventor wishes to retain majority shareholding despite having minimal business acumen and zero financial resources. Perhaps the managers were asked to write the plan and begin working for no salary but were promised (or think they deserve) a stake in the future profits of the business, if indeed such profits ever materialize. The members of the management team may dispute their individual shareholdings vis-à-vis each other's, with at least one feeling that he or she has worked harder than the other(s) and that the initially allocated shares no longer are fair or appropriate. Finally, the investor who appears at the last minute to

TABLE 2.1. Reasons for Allocating Equity in Your Business

| | |
|---|---|
| Ownership of a strategic asset | The owner assigns the rights to a strategic asset (such as intellectual property) to the new venture in exchange for shares in the company. |
| Work performed without pay | Known as *sweat equity*, stock in the business is awarded to people to compensate for unpaid work (usually for the inventor, consultants, and/or the management team, but also employees). |
| Valuable contacts, reputations, and/or networks | Equity may be awarded to persons in exchange for access to their contacts, use of their names, and so forth. |
| Investors | Shares are allocated to investors for financial contributions made to the capital funding of the new venture. |
| Employees | Shares may be given to initial employees who work for little or no pay, and/or may be reserved for later allocation to managers and other key employees as performance-based bonuses in order to better align their incentives with those of the owners. |
| Customers | A customer may seek shares in the business to be assured of supplies of a necessary component. |
| Suppliers | Equity might be allocated to suppliers in exchange for better supply terms and delivery arrangements (such as just-in-time delivery). |

save the new venture from extinction, but demands a majority share of the equity, may be strongly resented by the founding partners, because all the investor had to offer was the money!

Calculation of the precise share of ownership in the new business that should be allocated to each party requires the concurrent solution of two issues. First, what is the market value of the activity or knowledge contributed and, second, what is the total value of the new venture at that point? Given numeric answers to these two questions, we could easily calculate the appropriate share of each contributor to the new venture's value, inasmuch as it would simply be the ratio of the first answer to the second.

But at the time, when the new venture team begins to coalesce around the discussion of a potential market opportunity, a reliable valuation of the embryonic company is not possible. Cash flows and risk exposure are merely speculative until after the completion of a thorough business-planning exercise, and thus the expected net present value of the company's cash flows cannot be reliably calculated. If the total value of the venture is not yet known, what proportion of total equity should be allocated as sweat equity for the completion of a comprehensive business plan that might otherwise cost, say, $25,000? Similarly, what share is the investor's $1 million capital infusion worth, or what share or dollar value should be placed on the inventor's flash of genius without which the venture would have nothing? These questions will be answered throughout this book. First, the respective contributions and claims on equity will be discussed in terms of a typical entrepreneurial venture.

THE INVENTOR

In the beginning the inventor owns it all. The flash of genius and the subsequent refinements, modifications, intellectual property protection, prototype development, market reactions, and so on, are usually jealously guarded and are viewed by the inventor as his or her investment in the future of the new product or service. Although typically developed with minimal cash outflows and perhaps even minimal opportunity cost, the intellectual property is nonetheless valued at "thousands of hours of my time" not to mention "outrageous legal and accounting fees" (a common reaction to a first encounter with a fee-charging professional).

After a series of rebuffs from bankers and venture capitalists, who will require a formal business plan before lending or investing any money, the inventor eventually will seek help from a business-planning consultant and discover that a formal business plan will cost $5,000 at the minimum for a quick plan,[1] to $50,000 or more for a thorough analysis that includes technical product or concept testing and market research.

The inventor has a choice: Either pay good money for a good business plan, give equity for it, or some combination of the two. For a more conscientious planning exercise, from a manager who is more committed to the future of the new enterprise, the inventor is well advised to seek an agreement with one or more entrepreneurial managers who will not only do the strategic planning (culminating in the formal business plan) but will also manage the launch and subsequent expansion of the business. Inasmuch as cash flow is typically restricted, an equity allocation may be preferred by the inventor, who realizes that "X% of something is better than 100% of nothing." (This is a difficult concept for some inventors to understand, as they struggle to hold onto 100% of the equity without achieving any material progress in the commercialization of their idea. It is hoped that they will realize the folly of this approach before the window of opportunity closes.) Adi Gamon, president and CEO of Carnelian, Inc., (a provider of publishing systems on the Internet) advises inventors and entrepreneurs that it is also a mistake to choose an investor based primarily on maintaining control. He proposes that it is far better to involve a quality investor who can increase your chance of success, even though it may cost more equity and possibly even control.[2]

---

To demonstrate this point we introduce two hypothetical entrepreneurs. Ken Adler and Kerrie Dyer were both facing an important decision—whether or not to accept an offer from a potential equity investor. Ken had spent 3 years working every weeknight and most weekends developing his prototype of a self-cleaning pool filter. In Ken's words "Yes, I need the money ($400,000) but I have spent too much of my personal energy, not to mention blood, sweat, and tears, in this company just to give almost half of the company away." Ken Adler rejected the investor's offer and still owns 100% of his company that now has debts of $75,000, with bankruptcy imminent.

Kerrie Dyer also had invested a lot of time and personal funds into developing her educational software company. The investor offered her $300,000 but demanded 51% of the company and therefore control. Kerrie now owns only 28% of her company (her ownership was further diluted through subsequent rounds of financing). Microsoft has made an offer to acquire the company for $4.75 million. Kerrie and the other owners plan to accept the deal and use some of their capital gain to pursue other opportunities.

---

THE BUSINESS PLANNER

So, we suppose that the inventor recognizes the need for someone to write a formal business plan. Consultants frequently are offered a minor share in the business by new ventures that are strapped for cash, in return for writing a formal and comprehensive business plan. Indeed, the most common reason for requiring a business plan is to attract funding from lenders or investors. When time is of the essence, this culminates in requests for quickly-executed (and potentially less thorough) business plans. Unfortunately, when the business is not under pressure for a cash infusion, the inventor or manager may feel that a business plan for strategic planning purposes is unnecessary, inasmuch as they often think they know everything about the product and its market but just have not had enough spare time to write it all down!

Before the business planners can argue for any cash payment or equity share of the business, they must convince the inventor that they will add value via the business-planning process. This process necessarily will involve a series of meetings intended to obtain product and market information from the inventor. As the discussions continue and the business plan develops, the planners should be able to convince the inventor that they have information, ideas, and contacts that will add value to the venture, and the inventor should become increasingly willing to concede an appropriate payment or share of the equity to the planning team.

But precisely what share of equity should go to the business planning team? Essentially, the market for business-planning services and the market for the new venture's output jointly should determine the appropriate share of equity. For example, in the market for business-planning services, a competitive tender to research and write the business plan might be, say, $25,000. After the completion of the business plan, the estimated net present value of the cash flows (over an appropriate horizon and discounted at an appropriate rate) might be, say, $500,000.[3] Accordingly, the appropriate share of equity going to the business planners would be 5%.

If payment for the business plan is to be in the form of an equity share, the business planner may wish to maintain contact with the new venture as part of the management team or as an advisor or board member. In this way, he or she may watch over his or her investment in the business and be in a position to offer advice to management, if the business seems to be heading in what he or she believes to be the wrong direction.

THE MANAGEMENT TEAM

There is a market for managers, and perhaps dozens of potential managers would vie for the chance to join this particular new venture, offering their services at a competitive salary rate. Two issues militate against the inventor hiring salaried professional managers, however. First, there is the usual cash flow problem. The new enterprise is most likely experiencing or expecting negative cash flows at this stage, and the inventor may be unable or unwilling to seek more debt funding, which is not only relatively expensive at this stage but also aggravates the cash flow problem by requiring periodic repayments.

Second, the inventor may have a strong preference for the added incentive and commitment to the success of the business that comes from the manager's own involvement as equity partners. Although the professional manager's time can be valued at market rates, his or her commitment to the enterprise, resulting in additional vigor and diligence, is more difficult to evaluate. As with incentive remuneration schemes in the market for managers more generally, the management team may need to be provided with equity shares (or options) to induce the provision of long hours of hard work. But again, the market for managers will indicate the availability of suitable managers and the parameters of a competitive incentive package. The market for managers is like any other market for differentiated products or services.

The market for managers with secure employment can be tracked in the employment section of regional or national newspapers. This information also may be obtained from management employment agencies. Determining the premium that must be paid to the manager for undertaking a more risky task (i.e., managing a new venture) is more difficult to determine. Although this premium is theoretically applicable, the new venture should look for a manager who has appropriate attitudes toward risk, independence, and income,[4] that is, the premium required to compensate this qualified manager for undertaking the increased risk is minimal, given the potential returns. In the end, the equity to be given to a manager in lieu of work is negotiated between the owners of the business and the manager. The negotiated price is dependent on the manager's alternative forms of employment and the new venture's alternative sources of managers. Negotiating skill also may be a factor.

### Personality "Fit"

The issue of personality "fit" arises here. That is, the inventor and the management team should seriously consider how well they would work together before embarking on a long-term business relationship. This serves to limit the field, of course, and the inventor's decision to adopt a management team may be based more on a perceived personality fit, than it is on the management capabilities of the managers concerned. Such a trade-off nonetheless may be in the best interests of the new venture's long-term performance.

There is no easy answer in determining whether a personality fit will be forthcoming. You should be prepared to engage in a "courtship" with the investor. This process is similar to determining whether your boyfriend or girlfriend is the right person with whom to spend the rest of your life. You are facing a similar question when deciding on an investor—can I work with this investor over an extended period and under trying circumstances? When the investor is a family member, you already should have considerable knowledge regarding his or her personality and whether you will be able to get along. If the investor is not a family member, you need to get to know this person by spending time with him or her in different contexts (inside the office, at the factory or retail premises, having dinner together, etc.). Socializing with the investor should complement, not substitute for, your other due diligence efforts to determine the appropriateness of that particular investor.

## THE INVESTOR

The external investor typically is a venture capitalist or business angel willing to put funds at risk in return for a share in the equity in the business. All too often the inventor, the management team, or both neglect or postpone their search for an investor and suddenly find themselves in the iniquitous position of having only a single investor at the 11th hour, when insolvency is imminent.

In such circumstances (namely, facing a monopoly supplier of funds) the new venture can expect to be exploited to the maximum extent possible in terms of the amount of equity the entrepeneur must give up. The investor typically will ask for a majority share (51% or more) so he or she may take control of the venture if the management team appears unable to achieve the results promised in the business plan, and/or seems to be putting the investor's funds in excessive jeopardy. As long as there are any profits left in it for the inventor and management team, they may, if desperate enough, acquiesce to this demand in order to secure the funds but will feel as though they have been held to ransom. Alternatively, the investor may accept a smaller share of equity plus a "call option" on at least some part of management's equity.

The *call option* allows the investor (at predetermined times or triggered by failure to reach predetermined performance levels) to increase his or her shareholding. This increase in the investor's ownership of the business may even provide the investor voting control of the business, that is, the call option specifically may have been designed so that control is transferred from management (inventor and management team, assuming they are majority owners) to the investor, if management fails to achieve particular profit or other target outcomes "promised" in the business plan.

The use of a call option may be an attractive feature for both management and investors. If management performs as expected, then management is able to maintain control, and the investor has matched or exceeded his or her expected return on investment. But, if performance fails to meet a minimum level (specified in the investment relationship) then the investor is able to minimize his or her risks by taking control of the company and taking action to reverse the poor performance trend. Of course, a call option does not necessarily cause changes in control (for example, an investor may agree to increase his or her shareholding from 25% to 30% at the end of the third year regardless of performance), but the above demonstrates how the call option can be used to reduce an investor's risk and encourage him or her to invest in your business.

In theory, the investor's contribution is some proportion of the present value of the firm, and this proportion should equal the share of equity given up by the owners. But this will require agreement between the parties on production and marketing projections, the time horizon over which cash flows are counted, the discount rate, and the "end-of-horizon" value of the business. These issues, including the appropriate valuation of the business and the negotiation process required to achieve agreement on the valuation of the business and the equity share for the investor, are addressed in Chapter 8.

## RECOMMENDATIONS ON EQUITY ALLOCATION

We suggest seven main means to reduce the conflict arising among the parties to the new venture. Such measures will serve to increase the probability of new venture success by building appropriate incentive structures into the allocation decision. We suggest the following:

- Drawing up an agreed-on *ownership plan* for all shareholders of the new venture
- Allocating *sweat equity* in a sequential manner, only as people "earn" it
- Developing an explicit protocol for financial calls
- Establishing explicit criteria for external investors
- Establishing incentive contracts with stakeholders
- Using the market to obtain bargaining advantage
- Establishing an explicit understanding with investors concerning how involved they will be in the day-to-day management of the business

DRAW UP AN OWNERSHIP PLAN

All parties to the equity allocation decision ideally should agree on a long-term *ownership plan* that is in place at the time they join the group, such that their joining is subject to the conditions specified in the plan. Alternatively, they may join on the basis of a negotiated variation from explicit conditions stated in the ownership plan.

In most practical situations, the new venture will have survived the planning stages before feeling any acute need for external funding. The think tanks and planning meetings should cost very little in terms of explicit cash outlays. The time and effort of the people involved may be rewarded by the allocation of *sweat equity* to the business planners and the management team. Any cash outlays may be treated as short-term loans to the business by the person meeting the expense.

The initial round of equity allocation typically is in exchange for the assignment into the company of intellectual property by the inventor and for sweat equity provided by the business planners and the managers (who may be the same person or persons). At this point, these parties would own 100% of the issued capital of the firm. Subsequently, when equity is issued to other parties, such as managers and investors, the relative shares of the preexisting shareholders will be diluted. Funding by external parties, and the subsequent dilution of existing sharehold-

TABLE 2.2.  The Ownership Plan

| Party | Initial Shares Held | Relative Shares | Call for Funding | New Stock Issued @ $1 | Total Stock After Funding | New Share of Ownership |
|---|---|---|---|---|---|---|
| Inventor | 80,000 | 80% | $80,000 | 80,000 | 160,000 | 53.33% |
| Planner | 5,000 | 5% | $5,000 | 5,000 | 10,000 | 3.33% |
| Manager | 15,000 | 15% | $15,000 | 15,000 | 30,000 | 10.00% |
| Investor | 0 | 0% | $100,000 | 100,000 | 100,000 | 33.33% |
| Totals | 100,000 | 100% | $200,000 | 200,000 | 300,000 | 100.00% |

ings, should be envisioned in the ownership plan and not come as a surprise to anybody involved in the business.

Modifications of the ownership plan would need majority agreement by the existing shareholders. Indeed, for general shareholder harmony and to protect the minor shareholders to a greater extent, a two-thirds (or even higher) majority may be specified in the ownership plan, the subsequent articles and memoranda of association, or both. Alternatively, the company may issue different classes of shares with differing voting rights to different parties. For example, investors may be issued class A shares that reflect, say, 75% ownership but only 50% voting rights, whereas the inventor and managers may own class B shares reflecting 25% ownership but 50% voting rights.

Nevertheless, to structure the business in such a way at the creation of the company and the establishment of the memoranda of association requires knowledge of the unknown and the unknowable. The difficulty in obtaining the right legal structure for the customized deal with an investor (which may be 5 years after incorporation) is eased by the possibility of modifying your memoranda of association. The key here is to seek legal and tax advice from professionals before the legal creation of the business and at the time a deal is being negotiated. We realize that this can be expensive and can place a strain on short-term cash flows, although an inappropriate legal structure can be costly in terms of fees to change it, forgone tax benefits, and deterrent to potential investors.

In Table 2.2 we show some details from a particular ownership plan that identifies the various types of shareholders and the shares initially issued in recognition of intellectual property transferred to the company and for sweat equity. Then, in the latter four columns, the impact on relative shareholdings of a financial call is demonstrated.

Further calls for funding may be planned for the same way. Note that the relative shareholdings of the inventor, planner, and manager are diluted as the result of bringing in an external investor. This would not occur, of course, if the existing parties were willing and able to provide all the funding required. Resort is made to external funding when the existing parties are unable to raise the required funding; because they want to spread the risk to other parties; because the investor also brings expertise, contacts, and credibility to the business; or any combination of these reasons.

The investor may attach conditions to his or her investment, which affect the ownership plan for future financial calls. For example, the investor might agree to contribute the $100,000 in Table 2.2 with the expectation that this should be a sufficient amount to launch the business into a self-sufficient foundation. Accordingly, the investor might require that any subsequent cash raisings dilute only the manager's share, for example, and leave the investor's share undiluted. Or the investor might provide the funds with a call option on at least some fraction of the manager's shares (and perhaps also the inventor's share) that is exercisable if management is unable to meet certain specified performance goals. In the event of managerial nonperformance, the investor would achieve majority control and thus would be able to install a new management team.[5]

Much of the ownership plan would be incorporated into a partnership agreement or the company's memoranda and articles of association, which should detail the expectations and obligations of each owner. In perhaps most cases, however, the formal establishment of the business entity takes place some considerable time after the informal or de facto agreements are made between and among the people who will ultimately become shareholders (or partners) in the business. To avoid problems and minimize conflict, it is imperative to have an ownership plan in place (and evolving) from the outset, such that the partnership agreement or the memoranda and articles of association flow as a natural consequence of that plan. If not, there is the substantial risk that conditions and ownership shares may be imposed that some parties might consider not

TABLE 2.3. Sequential Allocation of Sweat Equity to Managers

| Timing | After initial discussions | 6 weeks later | 3 months later | 6 months later | 12 months later |
|---|---|---|---|---|---|
| Phase | Introductory | Planning | Research | Networking | Contract procurement |
| Progressive allocation of equity | 0% | 25% | 15% | 10% | 50% |
| Expected deliverables | Enthusiasm and initial ideas for strategy, marketing, follow-on products, and so on | Completion of business plan, with market research plan specified | Completion of market research, product testing, and intellectual property protection in process | Contacts made with potential customers, suppliers, manufacturers, distributors, and so on | Contracts signed with third parties to purchase, manufacture, and/or distribute the product or service |

in accord with prior informal agreements made, understood to be made, or both.

## SEQUENTIAL ALLOCATION OF SWEAT EQUITY

Our second major recommendation is that the ownership plan should set out a series of targets and goals that are designed to trigger the allocation of the shares (to be awarded for *sweat equity*) in a series of increments over time. Distributing the entire amount initially, and then expecting all recipients to meet their performance expectations is liable to disappoint the inventor (in particular), inasmuch as an effective incentive structure to induce appropriate managerial performance may be lacking. Thus, the inventor, planners, and managers should set out a schedule of equity allocations that will take place and add up to the specified shareholding for each party if and when a series of performance expectations are met at prescribed points in time. Table 2.3 offers a hypothetical example of the equity distribution plan for a person who is undertaking both the planning and management roles in a particular company.

Note that the percentages in Table 2.3 add to 100%. Thus, the share that the ownership plan provides for the planning and management team (20% in the example of Table 2.2) would be distributed in parts, starting with 5% (that is, 25% of 20%) on completion of a satisfactory business plan and so on. If the inventor feels that management failed to provide a satisfactory business plan, he or she would prevent the distribution of these shares, assuming the inventor holds the majority share. In some cases, one or more investors already will be involved at this stage and, therefore, also would be involved in the issue of whether or not the business plan is satisfactory, or an outside arbitrator might be appointed.

This sequential allocation of the agreed share is easier for the inventor to accept when it is agreed to in advance, as it operates as both a carrot and a stick for the managers. If they perform up to the inventor's expectations (which should be stated explicitly as part of the contract between the parties) they will be assigned a specified part of the total share in each stage of the development of the business.

### Dispute Resolution

The performance criteria for the managers must be externally meas-urable and not be simply whether or not the inventor is "happy with" the managers, because it may well be that substantial differences of opinion arise as the management team takes the inventor's "baby" down the road to market. The inventor's personal preferences and biases may not be in the best interests of the other shareholders. If such disputes arise, it will be the opinion of the majority shareholders, which will ultimately prevail, of course. But settling disputes in this manner may result in the outvoted party withdrawing from the business to the detri-ment of that business. A more amicable settlement may be found if the parties use an external party (such as a professional consulting firm) as an arbitrator, with the identity of this party being agreed on in advance.

### DEVELOP AN EXPLICIT PROTOCOL
### FOR FINANCIAL CALLS

An explicit protocol for financial calls should be part of the firm's long-term ownership plan. As an example, parties may agree that calls for financial input first should be offered to existing shareholders. Further, the funding required at a particular time might be apportioned across the existing shareholders in proportion to their relative shareholdings. Those meeting the call would be issued a commensurate number of new shares. If any shareholder were unable or unwilling to meet the call, his or her new shares would be allocated to whichever shareholders are willing and able to make that payment as well. Failing that, investment or loans from an external party will be necessitated.

But which of the existing parties, if any, has a priority right to meet the call in place of a fellow shareholder who is unable or unwilling to meet the call? Perhaps each of the other shareholders will want to increase his or her relative shareholding by meeting the other person's call as well. Some protocol must be stated and agreed to by all parties. One solution is that those who want to contribute to the unmet call would have equal rights to contribute, in which case that share parcel would be broken into equal parts and distributed accordingly. Alternatively, those who want to contribute might share the parcel in the ratio of their own shareholding to the total of their combined shareholdings.

Alternatively, the remaining shareholders might bid against each other for the entire parcel of shares, with the highest bidder prevailing. This has the advantage of allowing shareholders to increase their share of the business when they see it as a very good investment but may be considered undesirable because it upsets the "balance" of shares among the remaining shareholders, even though they each have met all financial calls as requested.

## ESTABLISH THE CRITERIA FOR EXTERNAL INVESTORS

In the event that no existing shareholder is able or willing to meet a particular call, external funding becomes necessary. The shareholders must agree on whether or not any external party will suffice or whether they have the right to veto the participation of particular external parties (such as old enemies?). Does the party who is unable to meet the call have the same veto right (over the identity of the external funder) as the others who have duly met their calls? Are competitors eligible to serve as external funders? Are there other requirements that must be met by external funders, such as the provision of market information, production expertise, network contacts, and so on?

These issues are best considered early, rather than in the heat of the moment when external funding has become urgent. Ideally, a queue of interested external funders would be established and their ranking agreed to by all parties to the need arising. These potential financiers must be "kept warm"—that is, kept informed about the progress of the business, such that they still will be interested in investing when the time comes to call on them.

There is no single "best way" to develop an explicit protocol for financial calls, just as there is no "best way" to structure the relationship between individuals in an ownership plan; it depends on the personalities and status of all individuals. It is hoped that by working through the issues stated earlier, a mutually beneficial solution can be worked out.

INCENTIVE CONTRACTING
WITH OTHER STAKEHOLDERS

It is usually desirable to enter into performance contracts with managers and other employees that provide for the issue of parcels of shares at specified points in the future, if certain performance targets are attained. Such incentive contracts serve to align the interests of the employees with those of the shareholders, namely, to maximize the value of the firm. These incentive contracts should enter the ownership plan, of course, and should be known to all parties to that plan. Again, incoming managers, employees, or investors may negotiate changes in the ownership plan that are agreeable to the majority of the existing shareholders.

Other stakeholders, such as external suppliers and customers, also may be regarded as potential shareholders in the new venture's ownership plan. Strategic alliances with major suppliers may serve to ensure the availability of supplies of critical components and also provide an additional incentive for the maintenance and monitoring of high-quality items being supplied. Negotiated terms with a supplier, such as a moratorium on payment for supplies for 90 days, might allow the new business to avoid a cash flow crisis and thus is worth a modest equity share in the new business.

Similarly, a strategic alliance with a major customer may ensure the retention of that customer and thus maintain revenue stability, inasmuch as dividend income to shareholders will reduce the effective price of the product or service supplied to that customer. Such alliances might include an agreement to make payment in advance, pay half the price when the order is half filled, or cash within 7 days, which provides cash flow advantages to the new business.

## LET THE MARKET WORK FOR YOU

It is critically important to use market forces to drive the cost of equity or loan funding down to a competitive rate. Management must not wait too long before seeking funding; rather, forward planning must be constantly done to identify the need for funding well in advance. Instead of desperately seeking funding at the 11th hour, management should line up several potential funding parties well before the need for such funding becomes urgent and seek the best deal from those offered. In essence, the new venture must avoid placing itself in a situation in which monopoly exploitation by an investor becomes inevitable.

## AGREE ON THE INVESTOR'S INVOLVEMENT IN THE BUSINESS

Entrepreneurs often are annoyed and frustrated by the unanticipated surveillance they and their business receive from the investor after the funds are committed. It is only natural that investors, whether they be family, friends, angels, or venture capitalists, will want to monitor the progress of the business and satisfy themselves that their money is being put to good use and that things are turning out the way they were promised in the business plan. Worse, some entrepreneurs find that the investor is constantly interfering in the business, meddling in production or sales, and arguing over management decisions.

To avoid such undesirable outcomes, which can lead to the breakdown of the relationship between the entrepreneur and the investor and jeopardize the availability of further funding, it is a good idea to agree explicitly with the investor on what his or her role will be. First, if the investor has little else to offer except the money, perhaps it should be recognized explicitly that the investor is to be regarded as a passive investor and is not entitled to arrive unannounced on the premises and take management's time with discussion of the business and related issues.

Such investors must be kept informed of course, but there are plenty of mechanisms to achieve this. Shareholder meetings can be arranged annually, quarterly, or even monthly, if required. The board of directors will meet more frequently, perhaps, and each represents a constituency to whom he or she should report regularly. A newsletter can be produced by clerical staff (with managerial guidance) for distribution to investors on a monthly basis. It is a good idea to send this newsletter to your bank manager and to potential investors as well, to "keep them warm" in case you need more funding later. Short phone conversations with passive investors should be tolerated, even welcomed, for the same reason.

Investors who offer more than money, such as managerial experience, supplier or customer relationships, industry or financial contacts, and other networks, should be treated somewhat differently. They should be told they are always welcome to visit the business (it is hoped that they will be too busy to make a nuisance of themselves!). The entrepreneur can schedule and structure these visits to suit his or her own schedule, by inviting all such investors on a particular day for a plant tour and a presentation on the current state of the business.

Essentially, the entrepreneur's and the investor's expectations need to be aligned with respect to an "active" investor's degree of activity in the business. The entrepreneur needs to make it explicit that although the active investor is always welcome to visit, managerial time may not be available unless the visit is scheduled in advance (at a convenient time). To the extent that such expectations are written down and understood, the relationship between active investor and the entrepreneur should proceed all the more smoothly. From the investor's viewpoint, an explicit (positive) statement concerning his or her access to management and the desirability of investor input may serve to reduce anxieties the investor might have about insufficient access to management or to the business, to monitor the performance of management and the security of his or her investment.

CONSULT AN ATTORNEY

In this book, we do not consider the legal form your business should adopt, and we recommend that you seek such advice from an attorney. Alternatives include a corporation, an S-corporation, a limited liability partnership, or a simple partnership (or a sole proprietorship if you share the equity with nobody). There are different implications for tax and personal liabilities in each situation.

Too often companies are formed without sufficient thought for the future owners, especially the raising of equity capital. An entrepreneur needs to be aware of the issues detailed in this book and consult an attorney. We realize, particularly in the early years, that attorney fees place a significant strain on cash flow. Nevertheless, the "correct" legal structure can provide enormous returns to the business and individual owners through legal tax minimization and an increased ability to attract and incorporate investors.

## CONCLUSION

To avoid conflict and to provide a greater degree of certainty concerning the allocation of shares in a new venture, it is recommended that the initiator of the new venture (the inventor) prepare an ownership plan that would be presented to all parties, who are subsequently invited to join as shareholders. This plan should state explicitly the roles and expectation of the existing shareholders but might nevertheless be changed after negotiation with incoming shareholders. The potential dilution of the initial shareholdings by subsequent issue of stock to consultants, managers, investors, suppliers, customers, and employees should be foreseen as far as possible and fully understood by all parties.

When sweat equity is to be allocated to those who have contributed to the new venture's planning and launch phases, a process of sequential allocation of parcels of stock (on delivery of measurable outcomes) is recommended. Under this process, the business planners and managers would be rewarded for their actual performance as time passes, rather than simply their promise of performance at the beginning of the process.

All parties must agree to a protocol for financial calls. As a typical situation, shareholders would be invited to contribute (within, say, 30 days) to financial calls in exact proportion to their share of the issued stock in the business. In return for such financial contributions, they would receive new shares allocated among shareholders in proportion to their financial contributions. If one or more party is unable or unwilling to meet this call, any of the remaining shareholders may meet this call, or the remaining shareholders may meet the call jointly and divide the parcel of shares involved in the ratios implied by their previous shareholdings.

Any restrictions and veto rights concerning the identity of external funders should be stated explicitly in the ownership plan and thus agreed to by all parties. Ideally, a ranking of interested parties who have expressed a desire to gain a shareholding would be established and these parties kept on a standby basis until their involvement is needed.

Next, the new venture must avoid monopoly exploitation by a single supplier of capital. The management team must seek competitive tenders for funds well in advance of the need becoming urgent. By attracting multiple potential investors for the equity funding, the firm should be able to get more than the money—it should be able to choose among potential funders on the basis of nonmonetary factors such as interest and expertise in the field of business, contacts, and networks, preferred personality fit, and so on.

Finally, the entrepreneur should make an explicit statement (preferably written as part of a letter before a deal is formalized, perhaps thanking the investor for his or her interest in investing in the business) concerning his or her expectations about the investor's access to the business and the desirability of constructive suggestions from the investor at appropriate times and places, that will help rather than hinder the smooth functioning of the business. If the investor disagrees, perhaps a mutually satisfactory compromise can be worked out, and in any case it is better to know sooner than later.

## NOTES

1. Of course, in some geographical locations, "fill-in-the-gap" type business plans can be prepared for as little as $1,000 to $1,500.

2. Garner, R. (1997, September 29). Looking for cash? You may not need to go far. *Computer World,* p. 14.

3. Issues related to establishing the appropriate time horizon and discount rate are detailed in Chapter 8.

4. Douglas, E. J., & Shepherd, D. A. (1997). *Entrepreneurship as a utility maximizing response* (Discussion Paper #97-91, General Motors Research Center for Strategy in Management). Evanston, IL: Northwestern University, J. L. Kellogg Graduate School of Management.

5. Table 2.2 is perhaps not typical in that it shows the inventor providing a major part of the launch funding. Many inventors find themselves cash poor by the time the launch of the new venture approaches and thus are unable to meet any substantial financial call. The dilution of the inventor's share (and perhaps also the planner's and the manager's shares) due to inability to meet the financial call is discussed later under the third recommendation, develop an explicit protocol for financial calls.

# 3 | Evaluate the Business From the Investor's Perspective

In the preceding chapters, we discussed the sources of possible funding for a new venture and the importance of "getting your house in order" in terms of equity allocation and the expected roles of owners and managers. Before we discuss the means of communicating the business to an investor we need to be aware of what investors will be looking for when they evaluate potential investments.

Understanding what investors are looking for will help the entrepreneur better describe the new venture in terms of what the investor would see as strengths of the venture and, at the same time, deemphasize those aspects that the investor may see as weaknesses. This chapter provides advice on how the entrepreneur can display his or her new venture in the best possible light. We discuss different types of new ventures and indicate which types of ventures are more likely to attract venture capital or business angel's funds and those that will be confined solely to "inventor, family, and friends'" funds.

The investor also will be concerned about the risk that the new venture may fail and go out of business. In principle, this risk can be traced to lack of information on the part of three main groups, namely (a) customers, who may know very little about the product being offered; (b) the producer, who may have to learn new manufacturing technologies; and (c) the managers, who may not be aware of the best management practices available. The investor needs to be convinced that initial ignorance in any of these dimensions will not be fatal, and that the management team can reduce ignorance by adopting specific risk reduction strategies.

## WHAT ARE INVESTORS LOOKING FOR?

Investors are looking for new ventures that "score" on most, if not all, of the following checklist points:

- Does it fit within the domain of the investor's knowledge and experience?
- Does the new product or service offer superior value?
- Does it serve a long-felt need?
- Does the new venture hold a proprietary position?
- Will the new venture grow by rolling out new products, new markets, or both?
- Is there already some hard evidence that the business will be a success?

### NEW VENTURES WITHIN THE INVESTOR'S DOMAIN

Whereas the selection criteria used by investors differ from one investor to the next, some new ventures have a better chance of obtaining funding from specific investors who have an interest in the particular area of the new venture. Put another way, the product or technology needs to be understandable to the investor so that he or she can feel comfortable and familiar with the problems of the existing products and can easily conceptualize the new product's benefits. Remember that an investor is unlikely to invest unless he or she feels comfortable with the organization, product or service, and the new venture's business environment. Some may say that familiarizing an investor with the market opportunity and the industry is one of the functions of the business plan, presentation, and question-and-answer session; however, there is only so much these can accomplish. If the investor starts from a position of substantial ignorance about the industry, the technology, and/or the customers, then the communication effort required may be too great to be achievable by the entrepreneur in the time available. Therefore, the entrepreneur should target an investor who is familiar with and has knowledge of the industry in which the venture operates or plans to operate.

This may not be as easy as it sounds and sometimes represents a double-edged sword for the innovative entrepreneur. New ventures that plan to launch a brilliant and radical innovation that will revolutionize or create a new industry are by definition charting unknown territory. These pioneers may have difficulty obtaining equity capital, because investors lack a frame of reference to be able to evaluate the business concept. Creating a frame of reference may be difficult to achieve. Under such circumstances, the entrepreneur needs to seek an investor with exceptional insight and "future think" capability, who has gained a reputation for supporting radical new ideas in disparate fields. An example of this is the investors who had the foresight to invest in Netscape, a free web-browsing service. Alternatively, you could consider a major customer (or supplier) as a potential investor, as they are more likely to see the benefit offered by a radical approach.

In general, the entrepreneur should target an investor in the same way that he or she would target a customer. You should choose an investor who has some knowledge in the field of business being proposed (or, for a pioneer, has knowledge in pioneering an industry). This is an advantage, because he or she more readily understands and feels comfortable with the environment in which the business is positioned. Also, because the entrepreneur should be looking at the investor as a strategic partner (i.e., someone who can add value over and above the capital invested), his or her experience, knowledge, insight, and contacts in the field of endeavor is likely to be a distinct benefit to the business.

NEW VENTURES THAT PROVIDE SUPERIOR VALUE

The investor looks for a new venture that adds superior value to customers, by which we mean that customers perceive your combination of quality and price to be superior to competitors' offerings. Therefore, the market offering must demonstrate either higher quality than competitors (e.g., bigger, shinier, more prestigious, more convenient, etc.) at the same price or cheaper than the competitors' products or services for the same level of quality. Investors are most interested in those ventures that can offer a product or service to the market that is superior in quality and lower in price yet still achieves a "healthy" profit.

The product or service must provide superior value for someone and, it is hoped, everyone in the value-added chain; that is, superior value for the consumer will, it is hoped, pull the product through the distribution channels, and/or superior value to the manufacturer will help push the product or service through to the end consumers.

---

For example, Breeze Technology Inc. has a proprietary ventilated footwear technology. This ventilated footwear technology offers superior value to customers by cooling the foot (or warming the foot in cool climates), providing superior cushioning, and being waterproof. Breeze Technology also offers superior value to manufacturers who are now able to make running shoes out of materials that are more durable and cheaper. Therefore, Breeze Technology is an example of a product (or series of products) that has the potential to provide superior value to customers through superior quality (and maybe even at a reduced price) and added value to manufacturers through superior margins (even if a price reduction is provided to consumers).

---

A new venture that offers a premium quality product at a higher price (higher price necessitated by higher costs) may find it more difficult to obtain investor interest, even though they may be offering value to customers. For example, imagine a luxury reclining chair that massages your back while you watch football. Lack of investor interest in such ventures may be due to the new venture's reliance on the top end of the market to pay significantly more for relatively minor product benefits and its vulnerability to competitors (existing or later followers) being able to find a way to do the same thing more cheaply.

Similarly, new ventures that closely imitate firms already in the market (a "me too" strategy) are less likely to generate investor enthusiasm and consequently less likely to receive funding. For example, an entrepreneur who plans to set up an ice cream shop (that closely mimics the operations and product range of Baskin and Robbins) in a mall that already has Häagen-Dazs and Ben and Jerry's is unlikely to generate a lot of investor excitement. A "me too" strategy typically does not provide superior value or serve a long-felt need or represent a proprietary position.

## NEW VENTURES THAT SERVE A LONG-FELT NEED

It is ideal if the product represents a solution to a long-felt and widely recognized need. If so, there will be widespread knowledge of the problem, and customers readily can see the benefits of the new product or service to solving this problem. For example, multinational corporations had a difficult time coordinating simultaneous communication with multiple businesses, using the telephone. There were many barriers to effective communication. Video conferences provided a solution to this problem. A new venture that provides a solution to such a long-felt problem more easily can convince an investor that demand exists and pioneering costs, such as educating and developing the market, can be minimized. Satisfying a long-felt need goes a long way toward convincing an investor that this business provides superior value over and above those products or services already on the market.

## A "PROPRIETARY" POSITION

Investors are looking for businesses that have a competitive advantage over competitors and for that advantage to be sustainable. To have a sustainable competitive advantage over competitors requires that the new venture have access to something unique (whether a unique product, unique production process, unique distributions system, etc.). A legally protected proprietary position can signal to an investor that the new venture has something unique to offer the market and that this uniqueness can be maintained over an extended period of time, that is, the law can assist by making it more difficult for competitors to imitate your market offering. Whereas investors are not so naive as to believe that a legally protected position automatically equates with high profitability, they do recognize that *intellectual property protection* (IPP) often provides important barriers to imitation. The ownership of protected intellectual property also signals to an investor that the management team has the ability to innovate and create something new. The ability to generate innovative products capable of achieving legal protection may represent a new venture's greatest distinctive competence and source of sustainable supernormal profits.

Investors usually are aware of the fallibility of any one form of IPP and will be looking to see if management has created a "web" of intellectual property protection. This web of IPP should be woven around patent applications, if possible, and should include the registration of all brand names, product names, logos and trade marks, and product designs, such that any imitator will become tangled in the web and be subject to legal action. Meanwhile, the managers should consciously try to build brand equity in these alternate forms of IPP, such that they offer protection, even if the patent applications fail or are subsequently invented around.

---

Coca-Cola has developed a web of intellectual property protection around their product, Coke. They have design patents on the unique shape of the bottles, registered trademarks protecting the brand name (Coke) and company name (Coca-Cola), as well as copyright protection. Coca-Cola uses secrecy to protect the recipe for Coke. Apparently only a few people know the recipe, and it is company policy that these people never travel on a plane together (in case of a plane crash). And KFC has a similar approach toward protecting its proprietary position, with one designated plant mixing the famous Colonel Sanders "seven secret herbs and spices" before shipping it to the franchisees.

---

Because the intellectual property inevitably will diffuse into public ownership over time, it must be supplemented with other competencies, strategic assets, or both. For example, building a positive reputation for not only the product but also for the business (i.e., the business's integrity, its focus on customer service and product quality, environmental protection, employment diversity, etc.), demonstrates to the investor that this new venture will be a hard act for others to follow. This is one of the reasons why investors are more reluctant to invest in service industries;

that is, by and large one cannot patent services, and imitation is often so quick as to provide little to no time for the innovator to build up reputation and brand equity.

## FOLLOW-UP PRODUCTS

Whereas the investors are looking for an exciting and profitable launch product, they are mindful that products can have a short life cycle and the party might soon be over. Thus, they prefer to see a series of products under development or waiting in the wings that can be rolled out in sequence as the business grows. Investors are not looking for a "one trick pony," that is, a company that is dependent on one product in one market.

If your product or service innovation stands alone, you may need to spend time working on applications of the concept to different markets, different models for different segments of the same market, and so on. Alternatively, or in addition, seek other products that are complementary to your main product. Thus, if your innovation is a new bicycle gear system, for example, you should think about application of this system to other markets, such as wheelchairs, as well as think about other products with utility to cyclists, such as improved seats, squeezable water bottles, protective jackets, and so on.

## POINTS ON THE SCOREBOARD

Investors are looking for a product that is tried and tested in the market. The entrepreneurs may be visionaries, but they should not expect investors to be willing to invest in a vision. Investors prefer not to take huge leaps of faith, and therefore anything the entrepreneur can do to minimize the leap of faith required will improve their chance of receiving funding (and probably at a better price). The most reassuring news to a doubtful investor is that the product already has sold 1,000 (or 1 million) units! When the market votes with its dollars, the doubts of the investor are substantially reduced.

If the entrepreneur can "bootstrap" his or her way through to the first sales, he or she will have a better chance of achieving investor funding for the business. First, this shows the entrepreneur's commitment and willingness to risk his or her own capital and, second, it demonstrates that the product does indeed enjoy market demand. Conversely, it may reveal that demand for the product is rather weak and/or that there are still problems with the design of the product, both of which are desirable to know before the entrepreneur faces the critical and experienced eye of an investor.

If not prior sales, what about confirmed orders? These indicate keen customers who are willing to pay for the product as soon as you can deliver it. Similarly, letters of intent to buy one or more of the products once it goes into production are better than no evidence at all that customers will buy the product, but after all, you cannot bank such letters.

Market research results are the next best thing. You will need to explain your research process, produce a copy of your questionnaire (or survey instrument), and analyze and summarize all the responses in a professional manner. The investor may be skeptical about such market research, because many investors have been misled by desperate entrepreneurs who do their research on "friendly" subjects, rather than conduct market research at arm's length, with a proper cross section of the potential market.

## THE LIABILITY OF NEWNESS

The liability of newness explains why new ventures have a greater likelihood of failure when young than they do when they are more mature. The degree of newness arises from novelty in three very important areas, namely, novelty to customers, novelty to producer, and novelty to management.[1] Each is now described, followed by strategies for reducing a new venture's risk of failure.

### NOVELTY TO THE CUSTOMER

*Novelty to customer* concerns the degree to which the market perceives the product or service as something new and unfamiliar. When customer ignorance is high, the product or service is novel to customers and there will be greater uncertainty over demand (and this contributes to an investor's concerns over business viability). Even if customers recognize that the new product might serve their needs, consumers may exhibit "quality risk aversion" and stay with known products, rather than risk their money on the new product that may not actually live up to their quality expectations or to the quality claims made by suppliers.[2]

---

The personal computer was highly novel to the market when it was first introduced. Potential customers did not know how to use it, nor did they fully appreciate how it would serve their needs, and indeed many were unsure whether they had any needs that it could serve at all (better than did existing products, like typewriters and calculators).

---

Similarly, *switching* costs may deter product adoption if the extent of the future benefits of product use is not sufficiently clear to potential consumers. Whereas customers realized the potential benefits of microwave ovens, they were reluctant to switch from traditional ovens where they knew their recipes worked. Suppose that every year for Thanksgiving, I cook a turkey that is basted to perfection. How long would it take in a microwave oven? Would I be able to make the skin perfectly crisp? It would be a big risk trying a different cooking system because it could ruin our Thanksgiving dinner.

*Search Costs*

Stigler[3] introduced *search* to describe the process by which consumers seek information about product availability, quality, and prices. He noted that advertising by sellers is equivalent to a vast amount of information search activity on the part of buyers. Even in established markets, ongoing advertising is required because information previously obtained (about seller identity, location, quality, and price) becomes obsolete, and new consumers continue to enter that particular market in a more or less ignorant state.

For totally new products, there is no existing stock of customer information about the product and hence no customer-to-customer (word-of-mouth) information flow that lessens the need for promotion (including advertising). To remove customer ignorance about such products will require extraordinary expenditure on informative advertising and other promotional support. More important for new ventures, there is likely to be a relatively large variance around the necessary advertising expenditure required, because management may not be able to accurately assess the depth of customer ignorance regarding the product.

Potential customers are less likely to adopt a product for which they do not see a clear need; that does not seem to offer a satisfactory solution to their known needs; or that seems to involve quality risk, switching costs, or both. The entrepreneur must foresee expenditures on advertising to inform and persuade potential consumers that this new product does indeed serve their needs. Note that a product is less novel to the market if it is readily seen to be a satisfactory solution to a long-felt need, despite this need never having been served previously.

---

For example, there has long been a need in the public transportation industry for video security. Shawn Marcell, founder and president of Prima Facie Inc., was able to satisfy this long-felt need with an all-digital "black box" recorder with high-resolution video that provides surveillance for both inside and outside the vehicle. His company grew from no sales and four employees in 1994 to $65 million in sales and 30 employees in 1997.[4]

---

Nevertheless, whereas an innovative new venture may face high customer novelty (increasing the risk of failure), the innovative product or service also may represent a distinctive competence leading to a sustainable competitive advantage.

---

Alan Bright is an entrepreneur who has invented a game called FutureBall. It involves two teams of 15 that each sit inside a sphere (like a motorized pinball) with the goal of piloting their spinning spheres to the netted area at the end of a football field.

The clear plastic spheres are piloted using a joystick. The other team is attempting to reach the other end. Crashing and blocking are the primary tactics of the game.

Alan is working in conjunction with two robotic engineers to design and build the spheres. This sphere design may represent a distinctive competence (protected by forms of intellectual property protection). The true competitive advantage arising out of the design might be the recreational possibilities for disabled people providing access to beaches, trails, snow, (and not to mention FutureBall), that was previously inaccessible. The *Sun Sentinel* reported that Alan Bright has plans for a $300,000 prototype that should be finished within a year, depending on his success in raising further capital.[5]

---

Alan Bright, like all entrepreneurs seeking equity capital, must convince the investor that he is capable of capitalizing on the distinctive competence, at the same time reducing risks arising from customer novelty, that is, the business will remain alive long enough to realize its upside potential. The entrepreneur must minimize the impact of the risks derived from initial customer ignorance, via a series of risk reduction strategies that are detailed later in this chapter.

NOVELTY TO THE PRODUCER

This concerns the degree to which the producer (the manufacturer of the product, the person(s) delivering the services, or both) perceives the operation as new and unfamiliar. The more different or difficult it is to manufacture a new product, relative to making existing products, the more there will be novelty in production. For example, car windshields in which two layers of glass "sandwich" a layer of plastic, were quite novel in production compared to the previous plateglass technology. Similarly, lightweight plastic components to replace machine parts that traditionally have been made of metal, were initially novel to producers. One might anticipate relatively high costs of retooling, operator training, prototype development, and durability testing for such novel products, as well as unanticipated budget overruns due to problems with the new product's durability, longevity, aesthetics, and so on.

The risk of failure increases for a new venture that is unfamiliar with the production or operation process required to produce the product or service. For example, a product that requires a novel production process will probably require changes in materials, retooling of machinery, as well as creating and learning new processes. Each change introduces additional development expenditures and a relatively large variance (both anticipated and unanticipated) around planned budgets. These up-front costs typically place a strain on a new venture's resources. Expected savings in production time, materials, or both may well provoke and justify pursuit of such innovations, of course, quite apart from the demand impact of the new technology. That is, an innovation expected to reduce production costs without changing the nature of the product, is novel in production but not novel to consumers.

The entrepreneur must convince the investor that the novelty in production is a source of sustainable competitive advantage, that is, this source of uniqueness will add superior value and will be difficult for competitors to imitate. At the same time the entrepreneur must convince the investor that the business can overcome this liability of newness, that is, not fail before the upside returns have been realized. The entrepreneur must minimize the impact of the risks derived from novelty in production, by choosing risk reduction strategies that mitigate these risks. Strategies for reducing risks associated with novelty in production are detailed later.

## NOVELTY TO MANAGEMENT

A third type of ignorance that will concern an investor is ignorance of the management team to the best practices of managers in the relevant market and industry. We shall defer discussion of this issue until the next chapter, where we urge the entrepreneur to evaluate the management team (including themselves) from an investor's perspective.

## THE IMPACT OF RISK REDUCTION STRATEGIES
## ON CONSUMER IGNORANCE

Attempting to break into a market with a new product bearing a new brand name confers additional risks to survival, as compared with an established firm broadening its product line to include the same new product. Informative advertising, and perhaps personal selling, must be undertaken to disseminate information to consumers. Persuasive advertising must be undertaken to overcome the reluctance of potential customers to bear quality risk or switching costs. Thus, information dissemination to potential customers can be seen as a risk reduction activity because it serves to better inform them about the product or service and its benefits.

An alternative (or concurrent) risk reduction strategy may be to seek a marketing agreement with an existing firm, which would market the product either under their brand name or under their corporate umbrella more generally. Existing brand names and corporate logos confer information about the probable quality of the product, the quality of the service, and/or warranty associated with the product, and so on. Marketing a new product under the brand name, corporate logo of an existing and well-respected firm, or both will thus serve to reduce ignorance in the market place and allow the new venture to avoid substantial marketing costs. Thus, the new venture may seek a marketing agreement with a firm that has an appropriate "gap" in its product line and simply manufacture and sell the product to that other company, which in turn packages and markets the product as if it held all rights to it. This should serve to assure the consumer (to some extent) that the product is probably worth a trial because an established firm would not be expected to risk loss of equity in its brand name by endorsing an inferior product; that is, there may be a reduction in the switching costs.

---

Richard Sachs invented Deklok, a revolutionary fastener that fixes the planks to a deck without any visible nail holes. He faced a serious marketing problem, in that Deklok required a totally new approach to finishing a deck, and deck builders were reluctant to change their method of deck building. This reluctance was reinforced by the fact that the new product was coming from a new company with no brand name recognition: Deck builders were demonstratively unwilling to buy a new product from a company that they had never heard of. To alleviate this problem, Richard entered into a marketing agreement with a major hardware retail chain. The established brand name of the retail chain meant that customers perceived less risk in buying the product, because they had developed confidence in the quality of the retail chain's other products and this confidence had been transferred to the new deck fastener.

---

Licensing the intellectual property to an existing firm also serves to minimize the likelihood of failure, as the risks associated with educating and developing the market are shifted to the licensee, that is, the licensee must invest in marketing to inform and persuade customers that the new product serves their needs.

THE IMPACT OF RISK REDUCTION
STRATEGIES ON PRODUCER IGNORANCE

The manufacturing process that culminates in the production of the new product or service will require the prior assembly of raw materials, productive assets, personnel, and information, which cost money to purchase, hire, lease, rent, or otherwise acquire. Much of this outlay may need to be made up front, which exposes the new venture to increased risk of financial failure if some cost and revenues are incorrectly antici- pated. Licensing production rights to, or contracting for manufacture by, an established firm (rather than attempting to manufacture the product itself) is a means by which the new venture can reduce the risk of business failure. This strategy will avoid most of the major outlays (including learning expenses) that are necessary with a manufacturing strategy. Many biotechnology firms follow this strategy, given the high costs involved in obtaining final FDA approval, manufacture, and then distri- bution of the product.

Of course, there are downsides with a licensing strategy, such as a reduction in the upside potential (need to share more of the profit), the constant need to check quality, as well as possible legal disputes arising over intellectual property, the license agreement, or both. Education, training and hiring experienced production personnel, or poaching them from other firms, also will reduce producer ignorance.

*Combination Risk Reduction Strategies*

It is obvious, then, that some strategies reduce risk of failure by addressing the level of ignorance across all three dimensions. Allowing another firm to manufacture and market under license, for example, can reduce the negative impact on a new venture's performance derived from customer ignorance, producer ignorance, and management ignorance. Investors are aware that all new ventures face risks (a management team that proposes that their business does not face any risks will be perceived as naive). Risks to the business must be acknowledged and plans to minimize or reduce these risks stated.

## CONCLUSION

In this chapter, we have asked you to consider your business through the eyes of the investor. First, is the product or service in an area of the investor's expertise? If not, perhaps you are talking to the wrong investor. Recall that in Chapter 1 we advised you to seek out investors with a preference to invest in your particular product or service area, as this minimizes the risk of "investor ignorance."

Second, does the new product or service offer superior value, in the sense that it is either better or cheaper, and preferably both, than the things it would replace? If it is better, do enough people think so, or is it largely a matter of taste? Different designs may be considered better by a limited number of people in what amounts to a niche market, but without the economies of scale obtainable from long-production runs, you may be unable to reduce the price to a level customers consider "worth the effort of switching."

Third, does it serve a long-felt need? If it does, consumer ignorance is significantly reduced, making it easier to sell, because most consumers will immediately see the benefits of the new product or service. If it does not, the investor will worry that the cost of informing and persuading consumers of the new product benefits will be so large that a sufficient volume of sales will not be forthcoming, or followers will free-ride on your market development work.

Fourth, the investor wants to see how you plan to develop the business. Does the business have a series of follow-up products coming through the R&D process, or in prototype testing, and/or at market research stage, which will be ready for roll out as a follow-up to the launch product? Does the business have a series of follow-up markets that the new venture can target with its existing or new products? If so, the investor will have more confidence that, even if rival firms invade your market with similar or improved offerings, you will be able to move on to the next stage and leave rivals competing with each other with what are essentially obsolete products.

Fifth, it is preferable to hold a proprietary position in the market that you plan to enter. If rivals can immediately or quickly emulate your product or service, your initial advantage may be short-lived and may even represent a first-mover disadvantage. Patent protection, and other intellectual property protection, are barriers to imitation that investors typically desire. Simultaneously, the new firm should be attempting to build a reputation for a quality product and excellent service, which may provide medium- to long-term competitive advantages.

Sixth, the virtue of having "runs on the board" was discussed, as this provides tangible proof to the potential investor that consumer ignorance and producer ignorance (and manager ignorance, to be discussed in the next chapter) are at acceptably low levels.

Finally, the liability of newness, or the increased risk of failure of new ventures, was analyzed in terms of the risks that are inherent in ignorance. Novelty to the consumer and to the producer were considered in terms of the ignorance of those parties that would need to be overcome if the risk of failure is to be reduced. Various strategies, such as advertising and hiring experienced technicians and production workers, were considered as risk reduction strategies.

In the next chapter, we view the management team through the eyes of the investor and urge the entrepreneur to put together a management team that is impressive from an investor's viewpoint.

## NOTES

1. Douglas, E. J., & Shepherd, D. A. (1997, June). *New venture survival: Ignorance, external shocks and risk reduction strategies* (Journal of Best Papers, 42nd World Conference). San Diego, CA: University of San Diego, International Council for Small Business.

2. To the extent that the product's price is relatively low, quality risk is less important because the consumer can ascertain the true quality at relatively low cost by buying the product. Quality risk becomes a more significant barrier to adoption of a new product at higher price levels. See Schmalensee, R. (1982, June). Product differentiation advantages to pioneering brands. *American Economic Review, 72,* 159-180.

3. Stigler, G. J. (1961, January-February). The economics of information. *Journal of Political Economy, 69,* 213-225.

4. Browning, D. L. (1997, October 1). Outside influence. *Small Business News, 3*(10), 8.

5. Nolin, R. (1997, September 20). Inventor might be on a roll. Pompano man hoping FutureBall fulfills vision of athletic quality. *Sun Sentinel,* 1B, Florida.

# 4 | Evaluate the Managers From the Investor's Perspective

The eToys is a premier internet toy store that offers over 1,000 products over the World Wide Web (found at www.eToys.com). The eToys successfully raised financing from private investors in September 1997 and launched onto the market later that month. The founders of eToys are Toby Lenk, formerly corporate vice-president in strategic planning at the Walt Disney Company and Mr. Bill Gross, founder of Knowledge Adventure (a children's software company) and chairman of idealab! (an internet start-up incubator).[1] From the limited but impressive information provided here about the credentials of the founders, the reader will not be surprised that they were able to raise the funds necessary for initial launch.

Investors almost invariably believe that the best predictor of new venture survival and profit performance is the quality of the management team.[2] Understanding what investors mean by a high-quality management team will help the entrepreneur build a team that satisfies their expectations. It also will allow the entrepreneur to best package and present the team so as to engender investor confidence.

This chapter first discusses the investor's typical requirement of diverse but complementary functional skills among the management team. The skills that are most desirable are detailed. Second, the existence of relevant prior experience in the same or similar markets is a "big plus" for investors, because one of the most common reasons for new venture failure is management's inability to cope with the demands of managing the business in the particular market environment.[3]

Third, the investor will be interested in seeing contribution of "hurt" money by the management team. Money personally put at risk by the managers is very persuasive to investors, because it shows the intensity of their commitment, among other things (such as their previous earning capacity and their access to funds).

Fourth, the potential differences between owners and managers is explained in terms of the so-called "principal-agent problem," and explains why investors prefer the management team to be equity owners in the business. Fifth, the benefits and sources of "friends of the company," the board of directors, or both are discussed.

Finally, and as forecast in the preceding chapter, the investor will be concerned about whether the new venture is novel to the management team. Put another way, the investor will be worried about whether there is substantial management ignorance with respect to the best practical means of manufacturing and marketing of the new product or service.


## THE QUALITY OF THE MANAGEMENT TEAM

### DIVERSE AND COMPLEMENTARY SKILLS

Management of a new venture requires a broad range of management skills. The solo entrepreneur would need to simultaneously manage marketing and sales, finance and accounting, research and development, engineering and production, and human resource management, not to mention various other leadership and motivational skills he or she must possess to keep the new business headed toward success. This is a difficult if not impossible task for one individual and often is better achieved by an entrepreneurial team.

New ventures wishing to attract equity funding need to convince the investor that they have not only the breadth of managerial knowledge across the functional disciplines (marketing, finance, production, etc.) but also the depth of managerial talent within each discipline. This breadth and depth of management knowledge, experience, and talent must be sufficient to drive the new venture toward success, often under conditions of high uncertainty. After all, the new venture either is entering a competitive marketplace and will compete with other firms who are managed by teams of well-trained and experienced managers with specialist talents or sooner or later will be joined by new entrants who are managed by such teams.

Many new ventures are strong on the technical side but weak on the management side. For example, an engineer invents a new technology and decides to start his or her own business, rather than continue working for someone else. Just as it took one or more university courses and time to accumulate practical experience to become "good at" the technical side, one cannot expect to be particularly good at the management side without prior business education and management experience. Investors are loath to invest in a good technical person who wants to manage his or her own enterprise. Venture capitalists, in particular, often will provide the funds only on the condition that the entrepreneur hires professionally trained and experienced managers (who might be available through the venture capitalist's network). The hiring of managers as well as performance expectations coinciding with equity allocation were discussed in Chapter 2.

### A Good Leader

First and foremost, the investor will want to see a chief executive officer (CEO) with good general management skills, visionary leadership, and a strong instinct for strategic and entrepreneurial thinking. The CEO will need to be tough-minded, because hard decisions often must be made, and emotional thinking may lead to decisions that the new venture can ill afford. In the early stages of the new venture, the CEO will typically also take on the roles and responsibilities associated with one of the functional disciplines. For example, the CEO also might be the technical expert responsible for the product(s) development and production, the marketing or the financial expert, as well as fulfilling the traditional role of CEO.

### Marketing Expertise

Second, the investor will want to see a marketing expert on the entrepreneurial team, with advanced business school qualifications and experience in a market similar to the one in which the new venture plans to operate. The roles and responsibilities of the marketing manager include market research, market development, and marketing strategy. As implied before, these skills might be resident in the CEO or in a second person on the management team.

### Financial Expertise

Next, the investor will want to see a financial expert, preferably a qualified accountant with appropriate degrees and commercial experience. This individual helps the CEO keep the business on the appropriate financial path, ensuring that cash flow needs are carefully projected, that revenues are collected in a timely manner, and that expenses are kept within the budget wherever possible. Note, however, that in a relatively small new venture, which cannot afford to support more than a couple of managers initially, the accounting and financial service role might need to be outsourced, unless they are a "second string in the bow" of someone else in the management team.

### Specialist Expertise

Depending on the size of the new venture at the time of raising capital, the management team might be expanded to include one or more specialists, such as a lawyer, an engineer, a physicist, or whatever special needs the new venture might have. Alternatively, the firm could outsource these specialists on a part-time or contract basis if a full-time job for them cannot be justified.

### Complementary Skills and Experience

The investor will prefer to see a team composed of members who complement each other, with minimal duplication of skills. A management team that includes two or three marketing experts probably has redundant skills, and therefore the management team is more expensive than it needs to be. Similarly, having more than one accountant, computer expert, and a variety of other roles probably is going to be perceived as redundant and wasteful of salary dollars by the investor. It is not uncommon, however, as many new ventures are started by groups with common backgrounds and experience (such as three computer jocks who start an Internet service business or three colleagues in business school who did all their marketing classes together and jointly start a new business). Such management teams need to be aware that their composition may not be perceived as optimal by an investor, and it may prevent funding of the business unless the management team is streamlined.

This problem should be anticipated early in the life of the new venture and avoided through careful selection of the top management personnel by the lead entrepreneur. Even if a group of friends are involved in the start-up phase, and deserve sweat equity for their early efforts, they need not all be involved on the management team. They simply might be part owners and employees or even simply part owners and work elsewhere, because the business cannot (yet) support that many computer experts, marketers, accountants, or whatever.

The management team typically operates in an uncertain and stressful environment. Therefore, the investors also are interested in whether a group of well-qualified managers also can work together as a team. A track record of working together helps dissipate some of the investor's concerns.

RELEVANT EXPERIENCE

The success rate of new ventures is positively related to the extent of relevant prior experience the managers have had in the same or similar markets and in the same or similar production processes.[4] There is no substitute for experience in many cases. Experience is just another word for knowledge gained in a specific context. An experienced manager will have been through a similar situation before and will have learned from previous mistakes (it is hoped) and recognize opportunities that would not be obvious to neophytes.

Thus, investors find a considerable degree of comfort in the knowledge that the members of the management team have had sufficient relevant prior experience. If the management team is relatively "green" in terms of the market or industry they seek funding to enter, they might be well advised to add a member to the team who has relevant experience. If they cannot afford another senior manager, they might consider restructuring the management team to accommodate the inclusion of a more experienced manager.

## HURT MONEY

*Hurt money* is the self-financing provided by the management team. An investor will have greater confidence in the team if each of them has made a personal sacrifice in terms of financial contribution to the new venture. Oppositely, if the members of the management team have plenty of spare cash, have houses and other assets that are largely unencumbered by debt, and yet are not keen to invest a substantial part of their wealth in the new venture, what confidence would this give an investor? It would seem as if they want to play games with other people's money, they don't believe in the viability of the business, or both.

From an investor's perspective, if the management team has made a substantial financial commitment to the new venture, possibly all their personal wealth, this will induce the management team to work harder to protect their investment (and thus protect the investor's funds as well). Management's investment of hurt money even may provoke more creative thinking, when virtually their entire net worth is at stake.

## THE PRINCIPAL-AGENT PROBLEM

The *principal-agent problem* concerns the lack of incentive that employees (agents) have, to work in the best interests of their employer or owner (the principal). Agents do not have a claim on the residual profits; they only get salary or perhaps salary and a commission on sales. They thus have little financial incentive to make more profits rather than less, because all the profits accrue to the equity holders.

Principal-agent theory states that to induce behavior from agents that best serves the objectives of the principal, the incentives of the agent must be aligned with those of the principal. Giving the agent a share of the profits best does this, either as a bonus (which is a share of profits) or as dividends on equity held (which also amounts to a share of profits). In this way, the agent acts more like an employer (owner) than an employee, and strives to maximize profits, because he or she gains additional income as a share of those profits.

In terms of the new venture-seeking funding, the investor is effectively the principal, putting forward funds in return for equity in the business. If the managers are simply employees, they would be agents, and might simply do as much as is necessary to hold their jobs, rather than work even harder to maximize the new venture's profits. By making sure the management team members also are equity holders, the investor effectively aligns their incentives with his or her own incentives. This alignment of incentives is the basis for an investor's preference for managers also to be owners of the new venture, rather than being simply hired managers. It also underlies the investor's preference for managers who have invested considerable hurt money.

BOARDS OF DIRECTORS

Also reflecting on the quality of the management team is the quality of the board of directors that the managers have assembled. If the managers have been able to convince high-profile, high-quality people to put their reputations at stake and serve on the board, the investor will be inclined to believe that the new venture must be a reasonably safe bet, because it must have been already given the "due diligence" treatment by these board members.

It also reflects well on the management team that they are prepared to have external people on the board of directors (which is not necessary for a nonpublic company), because it signals that they are prepared to seek other opinions and listen to advice. Many investors will have had unpleasant experiences with entrepreneurs who think they know everything and who are reluctant to take advice.

An impressive board of directors increases investor confidence, because collectively they add more talent, experience, and industry contacts to the strategic assets of the new business. Thus, the entrepreneur seeking investor funding first should consider recruiting a board of directors, to help strengthen his or her case. Eminent persons on the board also provide the new venture inexpensive strategic counsel, access to a network of people who can solve technical and financial problems, not to mention the external benefits in marketing and sales that flow from their prestige and personal brand name equity. The company may need to take out directors' insurance to indemnify these persons from a number of possible legal actions.

ADVISORY GROUPS

A similar source of inexpensive advice and other professional services
is to assemble a group of people who serve in an advisory capacity,
typically on a voluntary basis. Usually such groups are formed on the
basis of personal relationships: They are effectively "friends of the company" who share an interest in the company, the entrepreneurs, or both.
Ideally, the group should have a diverse set of skills, knowledge, experience, and networks.

Setting up such advisory groups avoids salary or retainer fees that
might be payable to a formal board of directors, at a time when the new
venture most needs to conserve its cash flow. This may include lawyers
and accountants who benefit from your continued business. Assembling
and using an advisory group impresses an investor, who might reason
that the entrepreneur must be a special person (or the business must be
especially interesting) if he or she can obtain agreement from such a
diverse group of people to serve in this capacity for little or no remuneration. Shawn Marcell, founder and president of Prima Facie Inc.,
which produces video surveillance equipment for the public transportation industry, believes his advisory board provided important guidance
in dealing with problems, provided an extensive network that helped him
"get in a lot of doors" that otherwise may have been closed, and helped
structure beneficial strategic partnerships.[5]


## NOVELTY TO MANAGEMENT


As we saw in Chapter 3, *novelty to management* concerns the extent to
which managers of the firm have prior knowledge and experience with
managing the proposed product in the targeted market under projected
circumstances (or in any similar environments). We refer to management
as the way in which human and financial resources are managed to maximize the efficiency of producing and marketing the product. Management "best practice" would define the state-of-the-art management.

Novelty to management is the absence of management competency
in the context of this particular new product. It is the antithesis of "stick
to your knitting" and is exemplified by management trying to manage a

production process and the marketing of a product in which they have little or no prior experience or expertise.

When the new product or service is novel to the management team, managers will be more likely to waste resources, follow false leads, and otherwise make mistakes in the management of its production, financing, and marketing. Thus the cost of producing, financing, and marketing the new product will be higher with a greater variance for novice managers than it would have with managers who are more knowledgeable and experienced in the management of this particular (type of) product.

---

In the early 1990s, many new ventures were created around the world with the purpose of breeding the emu (which is a large, flightless native bird of Australia, similar to an ostrich) for its meat, its leather, and its feathers. Emu pairs were selling for in excess of $100,000. Many of these ventures failed because their founders lacked knowledge and experience within the product markets, and with the breeding (production) process. The founders of Emu Now, a Texas-based company, increased their knowledge about the product and potential markets by learning from Australian Aboriginals. They now have a range of emu products, including decorative emu eggs, hides, feathers, meats, and oils.[6] Thus, the risk of business failure for Emu Now (as for other businesses) can be significantly reduced by assembling a management team that has related experience and knowledge (or can rapidly obtain such knowledge) with the new product in the targeted environment.

---

The management team's related experience and knowledge must include competence in financial management, because the failure of so many new ventures is attributed to insufficient funding[7] (because costs were higher, or revenues lower, than expected). It is almost axiomatic to advise new ventures to begin with substantially more capital funding than they think they will need. This is particularly so when the firm is subject to rapid growth pressures. Good advice might be to fund for the worst scenario, after rethinking that scenario to ensure that it includes all of the things that could go wrong, including negative shocks, actually going wrong. New ventures thus should begin with access to a line of credit substantially larger than they expect to need for the most likely scenario.

Similarly, they should organize access to funds well before they expect to need the funds, because last-minute desperation for funds (in response to an unexpected negative shock, for example) may make those funds harder to obtain. Obtaining funds earlier than expected can help overcome unanticipated financial setbacks. Of course, securing funds early also has its costs, because the earlier funds are secured, the higher the discount rate that is usually applied—you need to give away more of the company to obtain the money. Discount rates and the calculation of equity to be allocated to investors is discussed in Chapter 8. Managing these sorts of trade-offs is an integral component of management competency. Conversely, the lack of management's knowledge as to when and how much funding will be required negatively affects the venture's chance of survival.

Other pertinent aspects of financial-management competency may include the decision to lease rather than buy productive assets, which tends to conserve what funding the venture does have for a longer period and thus more likely allows the firm to overcome any unanticipated revenue setbacks or cost overruns. It is similarly cash conserving to hire consultants rather than to employ specialists if the services of the full-time employee would be underused in the early stages of the venture. It also may be sound financial management to initially operate from a "home office" or to share a serviced office. Taking out insurance against the worst outcomes also may indicate sound financial management, assuming it reflects an assessment of the information on the costs and risks involved.

The information required to manage competently must be expected to vary with the complexity of the industry and with the competitiveness of the market. Some production processes are no doubt harder to manage than are others, owing to greater (or lesser) regulation and legislation affecting that industry. Further, the technical difficulty of some production processes differs, and the vulnerability to expensive mistakes will be greater in some industries. Similarly, more competitive markets will require managers to seek more information about customers, competitors, suppliers, employees, and stockholders than they need in less competitive markets. Thus, whereas investors rank the quality of the management team as the number one criterion they use in evaluating a new venture's viability, there is no absolute quantum of information required by managers for them to be regarded as competent managers. Nevertheless, there are steps that you can take to improve an investor's impression of your team, namely, risk reduction strategies for management ignorance (novelty to management).

## THE IMPACT OF RISK REDUCTION STRATEGIES ON NOVELTY TO MANAGEMENT

Management education and training and/or the poaching of managers with required skills and experience from other firms will directly diminish ignorance of best practice management. Successful entrepreneurs typically display management and business skills that include the ability to recognize market opportunities; the ability to mobilize people and resources; other leadership and people skills; and expertise in manufacturing, marketing, human resource development, and financial management. Such skills can be learned, further developed, or both via formal business education programs or short courses. To the extent that managers learn something new and pertinent to the situation at hand, management ignorance is reduced, which should in turn allow the downside risk of profit outcomes to be reduced, which in turn increases the probability of survival.

Insurance and cash conservation were discussed earlier in the context of financial management competency. These are, of course, risk reduction strategies that may obviate financial ruin in the aftermath of unexpected events that have an adverse impact on costs, revenues, or both, for example, an earthquake that damages a factory and severely reduces output for several months. Such decisions certainly require information (albeit estimates) of future costs and revenues, with particular reference to their expected magnitudes, variances, and timing. On the basis of such information received, competent financial managers either will insure and conserve cash balances or not.

Licensing or contracting the manufacture to an established firm shifts the consequences of management ignorance to the licensee and avoids the new venture having to learn much of the management technology.

The entrepreneurial team needs to convince the investors that the management of this business does not represent a novel situation or that it is less novel to them than existing and potential competitors; that is, they have the skills, knowledge, and experience to be able to successfully run this business. The investors want to know how this specific group of entrepreneurs adds value over and above the inventor. Communication to investors needs to demonstrate that the team has complementary skills, that is, qualifications and experience in accounting or finance; legal issues; marketing and strategic management; technical, engineering, or scientific knowledge in the relevant area; prior entrepreneurial start-up experience; and industry-related competence.

## CONCLUSION

In this chapter, we have considered the quality of the management team from the viewpoint of the potential investor. We first considered that the investor would prefer to see a diverse and complementary team of highly qualified managers, rather than an overrepresentation of some skills and a lack of other important managerial skills. We argued that the CEO should exhibit certain leadership skills and other properties and is supported by a chief marketing officer and a chief financial officer, if the business can afford it. If not, these and other specialist talents should be outsourced.

Management experience in a similar business is a very encouraging factor, as far as the investor is concerned. To the extent that the management team lacks experience in the business at hand, they should consider either hiring someone with that experience or delaying their search for funding until they gain the necessary experience.

Hurt money invested in the business by the management team also is an encouraging factor, because it demonstrates the managers' commitment to the new venture. It also serves to align the objectives of the managers (otherwise "agents") with those of the investor (the principal), such that the managers strive to maximize returns in the best interests of the stockholders.

A board of directors composed of eminent persons, and an advisory group composed of professional people like accountants, lawyers, and other "friends of the business," also serve to reduce the investor's anxiety levels.

Finally, we investigated the underlying cause of investor reluctance to invest in some new ventures, namely, those new ventures that have a management team that lacks important knowledge, skills, and experience in the particular market and industry under scrutiny. In this context, we considered several risk reduction strategies that serve to mitigate the risk of failure and, consequently, give the investor confidence that the new venture will succeed.

## NOTES

1. Sheehan, S. (1997, September 30). eToys, Premier Internet Toy Store, launches on the World Wide Web. *PR Newswire*, p. 1.

2. Muzyka, D., Birley, S., & Leleux, B. (1996). Trade-offs in the investment decisions of European venture capitalists. *Journal of Business Venturing, 11*(4), 273-288.

Shepherd, D. A. (1997). New venture entry strategy: An analysis of venture capitalists' profitability assessment. In P. D. Reynolds, W. D. Bygrave, N. M. Carter, P. Davidson, W. B. Gartner, C. M. Mason, & P. P. McDougall (Eds.), *Frontiers of entrepreneurship research* (pp. 566-578). Babson Park, MA: Babson College.

Shepherd, D. A., Ettenson, R., & Crouch, A. (in press). New venture strategy and profitability: A venture capitalist's assessment. *Journal of Business Venturing.*

3. Gorman, M., & Sahlman, W. A. (1986). What do venture capitalists do? In R. Ronstadt, J. A. Hornaday, R. Peterson, & K. H. Vesper (Eds.), *Frontiers of entrepreneurship research* (pp. 414-436). Wellesley, MA: Babson College.

4. Roure, J. B., & Madique, M. A. (1986). Linking prefunding factors and high-technology venture success: An exploratory study. *Journal of Business Venturing, 1*(3), 295-306.

Shepherd, D. A., Ettenson, R., & Crouch, A. (in press). New venture strategy and profitability: A venture capitalist's assessment. *Journal of Business Venturing.*

5. Browning, D. L. (1997, October 1). Outside influence. *Small Business News, 3*(10), 8.

6. Cook, L. J. (1997). Emu enterprise. *Houston Business Journal, 27*(20), S8.

7. Timmons, J. A. (1994). *New venture creation: Entrepreneurship for the 21st century* (4th ed.). Boston, MA: Irwin.

# 5 | The Three-Stage Communication Strategy

B rent O'Meara leaned back on his chair, placed his feet on the desk, and reflected on his good luck. He had just received the patent for a nonintrusive method of dissolving blood embolisms. Yet Brent realized that a brilliant invention, and even a patent, was useless without the money to develop, test, and then market the product. What he needed now was a strategy for communicating his excitement about the viability of the new venture, and the competence of the team that he had assembled, to potential investors. This communication exercise for entrepreneurs seeking equity capital is critical.

We propose a three-stage approach to this communication process. The first stage is the written business plan, which the investor will, it is hoped, read all the way through (and in detail if you are lucky!) The second stage is the verbal presentation (with audio-visual support), which you only will perform if the investor is impressed by your business plan. The third stage is the question-and-answer (Q&A) session that follows the presentation, and that will be longer or shorter, depending on the interest of the investor and the completeness of the business plan and presentation.

A STRATEGIC APPROACH
TO ACHIEVE YOUR OBJECTIVE

Entrepreneurs need to be strategic thinkers. They must know where they want to be and then devise a means of getting there. The same strategic approach should be applied to capital raising. The entrepreneur needs to be clear about what he or she wants from an investor and then set forth on a course of action that will give him or her the highest probability of achieving that objective. Therefore, start by asking, "what do you want from an investor?" Although every fund-raising effort is unique, there are some common objectives that entrepreneurs want to achieve and some common objectives investors want to achieve.

Both parties need to be aware of what the other wants and the priority they place on receiving it. By knowing the motivating influences operating on the investor, the entrepreneur is able to structure the communication process to obtain the best deal. The best deal is unlikely to be one in which the entrepreneur comes out of negotiations the winner and the investor the loser. This deal usually is not a "one-off" game and it is vital that both the entrepreneur and the investor come out of the negotiations as winners.

There is more to an entrepreneur-investor relationship than money. Other nonmonetary negotiation points may include issues of control, transference of risk, ego considerations, and emotional factors. The better the parties understand each other, the more likely they are able to establish a strategic alliance that will give the investor a great deal from his or her perspective (as it includes greater emphasis on those factors they prefer) and likewise for the entrepreneur.

Investors, especially venture capitalists and business angels, provide a valuable knowledge resource base as well as a sounding board for new ideas and new directions. If entrepreneurs only obtain money for equity out of the investors, then they have short-changed themselves. The collective minds of experts are likely to produce superior solutions to complex problems. This does not mean that decisions should be made by a committee but that obtaining more information and creativity can help business decision making.

A simple task that can be performed when preparing for a communication with an investor is to list at least five major benefits that your business would receive out of a strategic alliance with this particular investor. Then, list five benefits this investor would receive out of a strategic alliance with your business.

---

Oceanics Products (an Australian harvester of an edible seaweed called *hijiki*) used this approach to encourage Asian Foods Inc. (the major supplier of Asian foodstuffs in Australia) to invest in their business. The benefits accruing to Oceanics from entering into a relationship with Asian Foods Inc. are access to an extensive distribution system within the domestic market; access to distribution channels into Japan and Korea; a reputable brand name; knowledge of market demand (including product mix); and the money to fund growth. The benefits accruing to Asian Foods Inc. from entering into a relationship with Oceanics are access to the sole supplier of Australian hijiki (an exclusive government license); exclusive rights to sell this globally competitive product (lowest level of pollutants and counterseasonal to the northern hemisphere's markets); a management team that has experience in harvesting and preparing hijiki, as well as business knowledge and skills; Australian citizenship (only Australians are allowed to hold the license); and ownership in a company with high upside potential.

---

This approach seems simple, yet it keeps the important theme of seeking a mutually beneficial relationship uppermost in your mind throughout the process of writing, presenting, and interacting with an investor to raise equity capital.

The entrepreneur wants to form a strategic alliance with someone who will provide capital to fund growth. It is vital for the entrepreneur to establish a medium- to long-term relationship with their investors, as they are usually the source of subsequent rounds of financing. We need to look at what cards the investor can bring to the table so that the most mutually beneficial alliance results. Be creative in thinking of possible investor sources (beyond family and friends).

Write down a desired list of all the things that would help you build a highly successful business. It might include exclusive access to some raw materials, access to overseas distribution channels, and/or contacts in the government. Once this is done, the entrepreneur then must think of sources of these benefits. For example, forming a strategic alliance with the major distributor of complementary products may be a source of both the capital required and also vital access to major international markets. It is hoped that it also would provide important benefits to the investor. This would be a case of a "win-win" situation.

Now that we have an idea of what we want to achieve, we need to discuss how we are going to get there. The rest of this book addresses that question, that is, how does a new venture obtain equity capital through writing and presenting a business plan to potential investors?

## HOW TO GET THERE:
## THE THREE-STAGE COMMUNICATION APPROACH

Before going into the specifics of the message (the tactics), we need to have a broad course of action for communicating our message (the strategy). The strategy for communicating the message to investors involves three different methods of communication. Each method also has slightly different content in the message. The three methods of communicating with the investor are (a) the written business plan, (b) the formal presentation, and (c) the interactive Q&A session. Common themes running through each method are

- be clear on what you want to achieve in each stage,
- the importance of professionalism and parsimony,
- the logical flow of ideas, and
- building and maintaining investor interest.

### THE PURPOSE OF EACH STAGE

The purpose of each stage of communication is to provide the emphasis that puts the new venture in the best possible light. To be able to communicate the business and investment opportunity to investors, the entrepreneur must maintain investor attention and excitement throughout the entire process. To do this, the entrepreneur must provide the information investors require as well as dispel any doubts they may have. Unanswered doubts result in a new venture without funding. Therefore, the objectives of the communication strategy are to be aware and provide the investors with what they are looking for at each stage of the communication process, to decrease investor uncertainty, and lead them to the conclusion that the new venture is likely to be a success.

## STAGE I—THE BUSINESS PLAN

The investor wants to read about a proposal that jumps out from the page and captures his or her attention. According to G. Jackson Tankersley, founder and manager of a large venture capital fund, the purpose of a business plan is to get a meeting with an investor. This is achieved not through pretty colors or magic but with an exciting and professionally written business plan, not to mention an exciting business opportunity.

The ultimate goal of the business plan is to be placed in the investor's "Further Consideration" pile and not the "Rejection" pile. New venture equity investors may read a dozen business plans a week, typically many more. They have considerable choice. A badly written, badly thought-out business plan will be thrown in the "Rejection" pile, not necessarily because it is a bad business concept but because the entrepreneurs failed to impress the investor as managers—a good manager would not put forward a bad business plan.

The business plan sets out the foundation of the business. It should provide all the basic information the investor wants to know, without being a dry compendium of details. Finer details can be left to the presentation or the Q&A session. In Chapter 6, we discuss the critical elements of the business plan. It suffices to say here that the plan is the critical first step. There is no second and third stage if the first stage does not compel the investor to pick up the phone and invite you to come in and make a presentation. The business plan must make the new venture look viable, remunerative, and exciting.

## STAGE II—THE PRESENTATION

The investor uses the presentation to see the entrepreneurial faces behind the business that looked viable on paper. During the presentation, investors are as much assessing the management team as they are the business concept. The investors are thinking, "Are these people I can trust? Do they have the energy, brains, and commitment to work through the hard times and make this business successful? Do they inspire confidence? Can I see myself doing business with these people?" Therefore, the presentation must address these issues. Chapter 7 discusses in greater detail the presentation stage of the communication process.

## STAGE III—THE QUESTION-AND-ANSWER PERIOD

With the business plan concentrating on the business opportunity and the presentation focusing more on the management team, the Q & A session is the bringing together of the two. It is an opportunity for the investors to delve more deeply into the issues and the "nitty gritty" of the business and in so doing find out what the management team are really made of.

Although the presentation demonstrates the "sizzle," the Q & A session allows the investors to see if there is any "steak" in the management team, that is, does the management team have a depth of understanding and command of the situation? The Q&A session presents an opportunity for the management team to demonstrate that they know their stuff, that they are capable of grasping this opportunity and turning it into a successful business. It also provides a chance to indicate to the investors that the management team is knowledgeable and trustworthy and that both parties will benefit from a strategic alliance.

As will be discussed in Chapter 7, we advocate trying to anticipate the investor's questions and preparing "perfect answers" to these questions in advance. An immediate comeback with a detailed answer to a complex question certainly is likely to impress the investors. Going through several presentations in front of practice audiences will flush out most of the questions that are likely to arise, as will a few private sessions when the members of the management team ask each other questions they know the others do not yet have clear answers on.

*Strategic Omissions and
Inclusions in Each Stage*

The presentation should not be simply a verbal-audio-visual repeat of the written business plan. Nor would you expect the Q&A session to require repetition of material that was written in the business plan and perhaps also summarized in the presentation. You must forgive investors for their human fallibility—they read so many business plans that information overload causes them to forget aspects of your business and to ask questions that are well covered in the business plan and thus seem to indicate they haven't read the plan. Almost certainly they have read the plan. Unfortunately, they will have read perhaps a dozen more by the time your presentation is arranged.

Some things must be included in the business plan, although other things are optional—they might be deferred to the presentation. Some things might not be mentioned in either the business plan or the presentation, being strategically omitted such that they become certain questions the investor will ask. Make sure you have a thorough yet concise answer ready! Issues that are constantly evolving, such as prototype development and patent protection, can be left out of the plan because the information almost certainly would be obsolete within days. Yet be prepared to give an up-to-date picture of these issues in the presentation and expect more technical questions on these issues during the Q&A session.

BREVITY AND PARSIMONY

Anybody can be long-winded; it takes real talent to be brief and to the point. Investors are busy people with lots of other things they could be doing, although they are reading your plan or listening to your presentation. The opportunity cost of their time is high, so only a fool would waste their time with verbosity and redundancy and then ask for money, too!

The business plan must be 25 pages or less (excluding appendixes). If it is any longer, reading it will exceed the time quota that most investors will allocate to it. It should not be densely packed with turgid prose. Give them a clear pathway to stroll along, not a rock face to climb. They will want to read it in one quick session, form their opinion, and move on to the next one. Do not tempt them to give up and put your business plan down, inasmuch as they may not get back to it and days later will decide that if that plan could not hold their attention the first time, it is not worth further consideration.

The presentation should be 20 minutes or less, before throwing the session open to questions and answers. Remember, they have read the plan already and therefore do not need a complete reiteration. In Chapter 7, we indicate what should be presented and what details simply should be stated in the business plan. The presentation should address the questions they are likely to have (i.e., you must anticipate their questions) and the Q&A session is for questions you have strategically steered into the Q&A session, plus the odd question that is entirely unanticipated! Your answers to questions in the Q&A session also must be brief and parsimonious. Just give the answer to the question asked, not a 5-minute extension of your presentation.

## THE LOGICAL FLOW OF IDEAS

The business plan and the presentation can be viewed as building a house. In simplest terms, you need to establish the foundation, raise the walls, then finish it by adding the roof. Adding the roof before the walls are ready to support it surely will cause confusion. The investor would have all kinds of comments and questions springing to mind that are later settled when the missing elements are supplied. Meanwhile, he or she will have been worrying about those things rather than listening to your presentation.

It is surely better to take the investor through the plan (and later the presentation) in an orderly manner, each new part building upon the preceding parts, so that he or she more likely can arrive at the end with the sense of "no problems perceived" and have reached the conclusion that the business probably is viable. So, you need to think through the business plan and the presentation and ask yourself a series of questions: "Does it flow in a logical manner? What is the next thing the investor will want to know? What questions will this raise in the investor's mind?" And so on.

## BUILDING AND MAINTAINING INVESTOR INTEREST

In the business plan, page after page of prose can become tedious, and prose is not always the best means of communicating ideas or data. Visual aids, such as pictures or diagrams of the product or service concept, as well as charts and graphs sprinkled liberally throughout the plan, all serve to impart information in an almost instantaneous way and can be very economical of space. Tables allow presentation of data in an orderly way, such as the pros and cons of various alternative strategies. Such tables can be set in a font size somewhat smaller than the text and thus save page space and communicate more effectively.

In the presentation, it is similarly important to vary the pace. One person droning on for 20 minutes can be sleep inducing, especially if you have been up late the previous evening reading business plans! We advocate the use of a short video interlude (to best demonstrate how the product or service concept works, for example), more than one speaker, the use of graphs and charts interspersed with "bullet points" on over-head slides, and a host of other things to keep your presentation interesting. In Chapter 7, we provide more detail on this aspect of the presentation.

TARGET THE INTENDED AUDIENCE

Your business plan will be stored on disk and easily can be modified from day to day to include the latest developments in your business. It also can be modified to suit the target audience. You need a different version of the plan if you are trying to raise funds, compared with if you are trying to hire a key employee who (rightly so) wants to see the business plan to judge whether he or she should gamble his or her career on your business.

So, go through your business plan and make subtle changes in wording and perhaps content that you think will make a positive impact on the particular investor to whom you are about to send it. Similarly in the presentation, think it through in terms of what the target audience wants to know, and tailor the presentation accordingly.

CONCLUSION

In this chapter, we have considered some basic issues that must be thought about prior to writing the business plan. The purpose of the plan is to communicate with the investor the viability and excitement of your business and to secure that all-important second stage, the presentation. The main purpose of the presentation is to reinforce in the investor's mind the viability of the business and to impress the investor with the quality of the management team. The main purpose of the Q&A period is to tie up loose ends—to answer specific questions about aspects of the business—as well as to further impress the investors with your ability to respond to the questions asked.

Now we move ahead to Chapter 6 and consider the actual business plan, and in Chapter 7, we consider the presentation and the Q&A session.

# 6 | Write a Compelling Business Plan

There are many books devoted to the topic of "how to write a business plan" and this is not one of them. As noted in the Introduction, this book has a wider purpose, namely, *how to best present your business to an investor* to raise venture funding. Accordingly, in this chapter the emphasis is not on what material should be in the business plan but, rather, on the effective presentation of that material.

The first substantial contact the investor has with the entrepreneur and the new venture is through the written business plan. If the business plan fails to gain investor excitement, the entrepreneur is unlikely to receive the opportunity to make a presentation or answer any questions. For these reasons the written business plan is the most important stage of the entrepreneur's three-stage communication approach to the potential investor, which was detailed in Chapter 5.

A business plan is a description of what the business is currently and what it will look like in the future (usually the time horizon for the business plan is 5 years). It demonstrates the feasibility of the business concept, establishes performance objectives for the management team and communicates the expected role of an investor. The process of writing the business plan requires the entrepreneur to look objectively at all assumptions and to view the plan through the eyes of the investor, continually asking, "what else would I like to know if I were the investor?"

## THE VIRTUES OF PARSIMONY
## AND PERSISTENCE

Clarity and brevity are key issues in the writing style of your business plan. Clarity requires that the information be written in an organized way, that is, all information must flow in a logical sequence, answering questions that arise in the investor's mind just as these questions arise (or just before they arise). A logical flow of ideas is proposed in the next main section.

Clarity is helped by brevity. Brevity requires careful and ruthless editing. All members of the entrepreneurial team must leave their egos at the door and prepare to sacrifice beautiful word strings to the painful scalpel of parsimony. (See what we mean? That last phrase surely would be edited out). Redundancy is anathema to busy readers, although summary tables, charts, and bullet point lists are useful clarity aids to help reinforce major points, make the document more readable, or both.

## PERSISTENCE—KEEP REVISING
## UNTIL YOU RUN OUT OF TIME

The business plan is not a document that can be written in one sitting. It requires an interactive and iterative process. The biggest mistake an entrepreneurial team can make is to wait until they have all the information they require before writing. This is a mistake, because they will never have all the information they require, and they still will be trying to write the entire business plan the night before they send it to the investor. They may finish it, but it will lack the polish it needs to create a good impression.

Writing a good business plan is an iterative process. Start with major headings and subheadings. As research brings in information, include it under one of the headings. Make assumptions when information is lacking, and then replace broad information or assumptions with specific information once it has been acquired. Quite often, it is not immediately clear what research you need to do until you start evaluating the early drafts of a business plan. You read the draft plan and decide what other information you need to make the story more complete.

Think of the business plan as a painting. An artist does not start at the top left-hand corner and work his or her way to the bottom right-hand corner to complete the painting. The artist, in actuality, sketches out a rough outline on the canvas and then begins to fill in the finer details of the picture until (it is hoped) it communicates a powerful message. First, the background colors are applied, followed by progressively finer and finer brush strokes until the painting is complete. In fact, most artists will argue that they have never really finished a painting, that it could always do with improvement. The same goes for a business plan. There is usually more information that could have been collected and incorporated into the plan, if only you had more time.

## CRITICAL REVIEW BY AN OUTSIDE PARTY

At some stage in the process, the plan needs to be exposed to the cold reality of outside criticism. Although it may make perfect sense to you, it is important that the plan also communicates the desired message to a third party. Ask people to read your draft and make their comments. The people you should ask to read the business plan are fellow entrepreneurs who have successfully raised capital, accountants, bankers, and even past professors. It takes considerable time and effort to read and evaluate a business plan and such professionals as accountants may require payment. Up-front fees sometimes can be avoided if you can convince the accountant, lawyer, and/or banker that once the capital has been raised and the business is up and running they will be retained to service the company on an ongoing basis. This will be your first test to see how well you can sell yourself and your project.

Once you have been able to convince someone to evaluate your business plan, you must not be defensive or too proud. If they are asking a question, it must mean that issue is not completely clear in the plan (assuming the reader is reasonably aware of the industry and has reasonable business or investor skills).

In summary, the business plan is a "living document" that should grow and evolve every day. The final draft is simply a snapshot of the business at that point in time. It may be outdated as soon as it comes off the printer. No problem: If the plan makes it through the initial evaluation stage and you are invited to make a presentation, then the presentation can include recent developments that the entrepreneurial team has achieved since the plan was written.

THE USE OF VISUAL AIDS IN THE BUSINESS PLAN

The business plan must not be a solid block of words from cover-to-cover. It must include graphs, tables, pie charts, and bar charts to illustrate ideas, to reinforce points, and to break the monotony of the printed word. Just as "a picture is worth 1,000 words," these visual aids can help with your concern for brevity and parsimony. A bar chart or pie chart summarizes a lot of data in a form that can be easily and quickly understood. Similarly, a graph shows an upward trend in sales and profits more eloquently than a paragraph using the same space ever could.

Document design is important for the "approachability" of the business plan. Pages crammed with tightly packed lines of text do not invite reading. They intimidate the reader and cause the eyes to gloss over. A "reader-friendly" document entices the reader to read the paragraph and turn the page, luring the reader through the document while informing the reader of the message embodied in the document.

Font size and style is important. Some fonts are easier to read than others. And it surely would be a bad idea to use a font size so small that a 50-year-old venture capitalist is unable to read it on an aircraft because of the poor lighting and the fact that his or her glasses are in the overhead compartment. Use no smaller than 12-point font, except in tables and footnotes. If you want to pack in more information, choose a font style (like Times New Roman) that is easier to read despite being smaller (in 12-point) than other font styles.

First-, second-, and third-level headings should be in different font size (and perhaps even different font style), such that they communicate to the reader their function. First-level headings indicate a new section. Second-level heads indicate a major new idea (or subsection) within the same section. Third-level headings indicate a major new point to be made within the subsection. Using headings as part of the communication process allows the reader to keep track of where the writer is taking them.

White space is a good idea in a business plan. Leave an additional space before a new heading, and leave the bottom part of a page blank rather than start a new section there. Indeed, many people think it looks better and is more compelling to have main headings always fall at the top of a new page. This will require serious editing to achieve but will force you to consider the importance of every word and every sentence. Often, you will decide that this or that particular sentence is redundant, because it already has been said in one form or another.

Color always brightens up a business plan and also can be used as part of the communication process. For example, red traditionally means stop or danger, whereas green means go, or safe, and orange means caution. Blue is a cool color, whereas brown and yellow are warm colors, and so on. The use of color accents on the page, such as in a border or placement of your logo in the header or footer on each page, can be very effective. All headings, and header and footer separator lines, might be done in blue, for example, or in one of the main colors found in your logo. Just don't overdo it!

With an overall page limit on the business plan, say 25 pages, it is important to do a "page budget" before you start, and allocate a certain number of pages to each main topic. For example, the executive summary should be no more than two pages in length, and the financials must be at least six to eight pages, including the pro forma financial statements. A suggested structure for a business plan is detailed in the next section.

## CONTENT AND STRUCTURE
## OF THE BUSINESS PLAN

Although the content and structure of the business plan will differ from business to business, the following items represent the major components of most plans. Each will be addressed in turn, to a greater or lesser degree, keeping in mind our concern with communication rather than content. Table 6.1 provides a guide on the number of pages that should be devoted to each main section, assuming an overall length of 25 pages in the body of the plan, plus appendixes not exceeding about 15 pages. Suggestions on the contents of each section then are provided.

TABLE 6.1. A "Page Budget" for Your Business Plan

| Section | Content | Page Budget |
|---------|---------|-------------|
| 1 | Executive summary | 2 |
| 2 | Table of contents | 1 |
| 3 | Company overview | 1 |

TABLE 6.1. *Continued*

| Section | Content | Page Budget |
|---|---|---|
| 4 | New product (or service) concept | 2 |
| 5 | Window of opportunity and distinctive competence | 1 |
| 6 | Market environment and competitor analysis | 3 |
| 7 | Market positioning and competitive strategy | 3 |
| 8 | Manufacturing and operations | 1 |
| 9 | Research and development plan | 1 |
| 10 | Organization structure and ownership | 2 |
| 11 | Risk recognition and risk reduction strategies | 1 |
| 12 | Financial summary, assumptions, and scenarios | 2 |
| 13 | Pro forma financial statements | 4 |
| 14 | The "ask" and the "offer" | 1 |
| | *Subtotal* | $\overline{25}$ |
| 15 | Appendixes | 15 |
| | *Total* | $\overline{40}$ |

## THE EXECUTIVE SUMMARY

The executive summary is extremely important, and we shall deal with it in considerable detail. It is the first substantive contact the investor will have with your business. It must build interest and excitement. If it fails to encourage investors to keep reading, then they may stop reading and not express any interest in your business, as they usually have plenty of other business plans to read (and to invest in).

The executive summary must communicate a series of items to the prospective investor. Most important, it should first state the name of the company, the business it is in, and the purpose of this particular business plan. Here is an example of the opening paragraph in an executive summary.

---

*EcoClear Inc. has been established to globalize an innovative self-cleaning water filtration technology that is applicable to a wide range of markets. Our launch product is a self-cleaning filter*

*for domestic swimming pools, which has been successfully intro-*
*duced in the Australian market. This plan concerns the introduc-*
*tion of that product into the U.S. market and seeks $300,000*
*funding for working capital and continued R&D activity.*

In the next paragraph of the executive summary, the entrepreneur
needs to quickly establish the compelling benefits of the new product or
service. Here is an example.

*The strategic competitive advantages of the EcoClear technology*
*are its performance and cost benefits. The EcoClear pool filter*
*saves substantial maintenance time, water, pool chemicals, and*
*electricity, while consistently filtering to a higher level of water*
*clarity. EcoClear's simple design, smaller size, and low-pressure*
*operation also allows a substantial cost advantage in production.*
*These advantages are protected in the short to medium term by*
*intellectual property protection and will be sustained over the*
*longer term by brand name and reputation building and the fruits*
*of our ongoing R&D program.*

The next task is to establish the size of the potential market for the
new product or service and indicate your selected strategy to access this
market. Here is another example, this one for Breeze Technology's ventilated footwear.

*The market for athletic or casual footwear is huge. In the United*
*States alone, annual retail sales were $11.6 billion last year. Our*
*market research indicates that this market demands comfort,*
*performance, style, and value in their footwear, and is receptive*
*to new technology. The footwear ventilation and comfort system*
*of Breeze Technology Inc. satisfies these demands and is appli-*
*cable to virtually all footwear. Because there are several large*
*and powerful players in this market, Breeze will seek a strategic*
*alliance with one of the major athletic footwear manufacturers*
*who would manufacture and market the technology under a*
*limited global license. Breeze will retain the rights to application*

*of the technology in other footwear segments, such as military boots and dress shoes, and will continue its R&D activity geared to the application of the technology to these markets.*

Note that this paragraph also indicates the future products that are in the R&D pipeline. Next, having indicated the exciting market opportunity, the executive summary should indicate the qualifications and experience of the management team who are charged with managing that opportunity. Here is an example.

*The Breeze management team consists of Bob Brough, Peter Homan, and Tim Zwemer. Bob is a successful entrepreneur, having most recently sold his interest in a chain of themed video stores he cofounded and managed. He then went back to school and completed a law degree and MBA. Peter is a certified public accountant with experience with a big-six firm advising entrepreneurial businesses before undertaking his MBA. Tim is also a successful entrepreneur, having started and operated an engineering business before taking his MBA degree. The three worked together on team projects throughout their MBA program and bring together complementary skills and a wealth of experience in the management of new and growing businesses.*

Having asserted the market opportunity and the talents of the management team, it is time for a summary of the sales revenue, profit projections, and other pertinent financial details. Here is an example.

*Sales are expected to grow from $101,240 in 1998 to $5.3 million in 2002, based on conservative assumptions regarding market penetration and industry growth. Annual net profit after taxes is projected to grow from ($313,756) in the first year, to $2.4 million in 2002. Cash balances are positive throughout. The NPV of the business is $4.95 million after discounting all cash flows at 40%. The internal rate of return is 115%. The value of the company (assuming P/E = 10) is projected to be $23.8 million in 2002.*

Having described the company's business, its exciting new product, the talents of its management team, the extent of the market, the strategic option selected, and summary financial projections, it is time for the "ask" and the "offer." Here is an example.

---

*EcoClear is now seeking an equity partner with $300,000 and commercial knowledge of the North American swimming pool industry. This capital will be used to fund the launch of the company, its initial operating deficit, and ongoing R&D activity until net cash flows become positive. EcoClear offers the investor a 33% equity share in the company and pro rata representation on the board of directors. The investor can expect payback from dividend income alone in 3 years and would own equity valued at over $8 million in 2001. The projected NPV of the dividend stream and the Year 5 value of equity (discounted at 40%) is $1.4 million. This represents an IRR of 101% on the initial investment of $300,000. Put another way, the $8 million equity value at Year 5 means that the investor could recoup over 25 times the initial investment at that time.*

---

The executive summary then might conclude with a brief statement saying something like this.

---

*EcoClear Inc. represents an exciting and potentially very rewarding investment opportunity. The management team looks forward to discussions with you at your earliest opportunity.*

---

There needs to be considerable time and effort dedicated to the executive summary. It must not be a "cut-and-paste" job from other parts of the plan, that is, sentences in the executive summary should not be found intact in other parts of the plan. Write the executive summary in different words, avoiding the same word strings, to keep the plan "fresh" without annoying repetitions of sentences. This can be a difficult task for the primary author of the business plan. It may be desirable to have someone else on the team use their writing style to give the executive summary a slightly different feel.

COMPANY DESCRIPTION

The investor reads this section of the plan to obtain a brief overview of who and what the company is "about," that is, he or she needs to develop a "feel" for the company and to establish whether it fits within the category of businesses the investor wants to pursue. For example, investors typically have a preferred business stage, with some investors preferring new ventures in the seed stage (earliest stage), whereas others prefer the development stage and others invest only in management buy-outs. Some investors only invest in high-technology business whereas others only invest in certain industries, for example, telecommunications or software. As indicated in Chapter 1, the entrepreneur should find out what type of businesses the investor likes to invest in, before wasting time, effort, and emotion on a presentation that almost certainly will be rejected regardless of how viable the business promises to be.

It is important that this section of the plan is exciting, demonstrates a sustainable competitive advantage, and exudes professionalism. If the investor is excited after this section and eagerly reads on, then this section has performed its primary role. It does this by describing the business the proposed venture will be in, the window of opportunity, the principle activities, and the distinctive competencies that will lead to a sustainable competitive advantage.

WHAT BUSINESS IS THE NEW VENTURE IN?

The investor wants to know the management team's vision for the business, that is, what the company will be doing in 5, 10, or 20 years from now. The mission statement of the business needs to provide medium to long-term direction and at the same time not be so tightly defined as to constrain future growth, by placing narrow blinkers on opportunity searching. The investor's interest in the mission statement stems from the fact that investors invest in businesses, rather than invest in a product, because products will come and go, whereas a business may live on indefinitely. The following is an example of well-written mission statement:

*Oceanic Products' mission is to serve the employment and environmental protection needs of the local community, at the same time maximizing shareholder returns, by providing high-quality natural seafood products to a growing domestic and international market.*

Importance placed on the mission and the future form of the business should not be construed as a lack of emphasis on the launch product. If the launch product fails, there is unlikely to be a business left to grow into the one envisioned. Investors will see the launch product as the first test of the viability of the business and of the management team's competence.

## THE NEW PRODUCT OR SERVICE CONCEPT

Investors want to develop a "feel" for the launch product early in the business plan so that information about the environment can be applied (within the mind of the investor) directly to the product or service. Note that this sequencing of ideas is different from that espoused in most business schools, in which the environment must be surveyed first, unsatisfied demands identified, and a product developed to satisfy those needs. In the typical business-planning situation, a product has been developed and the investor wants to be introduced to the product first and then be convinced that it satisfies a real need in the market place. But note that, whereas investors ultimately will want to know the technical details of the invention, it is best to keep those for an appendix and concentrate at this point mainly on the product as a solution to a recognized problem.

*Oceanic Products' first product is hijiki, an edible seaweed that forms part of the staple diet of Japanese and other Asian cultures. Oceanic Products has the sole license to extract hijiki from the only known source of hijiki in Australian coastal waters. Hijiki is considered a weed infestation, because it is an introduced species that grows prolifically and interferes with boating and oceanic transport. It cannot be eradicated but can be controlled by annual harvesting. Whereas hijiki grown elsewhere absorbs dangerously high levels of ocean-borne pollutants, Oceanic Products' source is located in a wilderness coastal area, which is almost entirely free of pollutants. Pollution-free hijiki is in strong demand, not only by hotels, restaurants, airlines, and the local Asian population but also for export sale to Japan and Korea at premium prices.*

## WINDOW OF OPPORTUNITY
## AND DISTINCTIVE COMPETENCE

The plan must demonstrate that there is a window of opportunity and that the management team has the distinctive competence to capture that opportunity. The managers need to argue that the opportunity is real, not a mirage, and that they have at their disposal the resources and skill necessary to force the window open, grasp the opportunity, and capitalize on it sooner and better than can anyone else.

A window of opportunity implies that the business concept is a great idea and that the opportunity will not last long, before someone else grasps the opportunity. The investor wants to know what confluence of environmental conditions has incurred that has resulted in the opening of the window of opportunity. Describing the opportunity and why the window of opportunity has only recently opened (or, better yet, has only opened to the new venture) demonstrates to investors why *now* is the right time for the new venture and that *these* managers are the right team to do it.

The window of opportunity may of course slam shut, making the opportunity unavailable to the new venture and therefore the investor. There is an obvious trade-off for the entrepreneur (and investor). The entrepreneur, investor, or both might choose to wait for more information to reduce uncertainty and then make a better strategic (investment) decision, in which time the window of opportunity may have closed and opportunity lost. On the other hand, acting early on less information may result in the grasping of what might appear to be an opportunity, but that turns out to be an idea that is not technically possible or for which there is insufficient demand. Investors need to be convinced that all the information currently available has been included in the business plan, and even though there are things that are unknown and unknowable at this stage, they are acting on the best information available at that time. Here is an example of an argument that a window of opportunity exists.

*A number of factors have contributed to the window of opportunity opening now:*

- *The increased number of Japanese and Koreans working in and visiting Australia as tourists and on business has created a substantial domestic demand for edible seaweed.*

- *New legislation reducing the acceptable level of cadmium and arsenic pollutants in foodstuffs has almost totally restricted hijiki imports into Australia.*

- *Other legislation now prohibits discharge of bilge water from ocean vessels, so there will not be any new infestation of hijiki in Australian waters that could not be immediately eradicated.*

- *With growing public concern for the natural environment, "green" companies, such as those that control introduced weeds, can expect considerable public support.*

- *The present economic climate has led governments at all levels to be particularly supportive of new employment and export generators.*

- *An evolutionary change in diet has caused an increased demand for health and natural foods and fueled an increase in the popularity of Japanese and Korean food throughout the wider community.*

- *There is growing awareness of the health risk of polluted hijiki among the aging population in Japan, who have demonstrated their willingness and ability to pay premium prices for high-quality foodstuffs more generally.*

The investor also will be concerned with the distinctive competence of the new venture to grasp the opportunity and then close the window of opportunity to others. Successful businesses are based on sustainable competitive advantages, which are derived from a "fit" between the distinctive competencies of the venture and the environment in which they will be combined. Distinctive competence may reside in the firm's financial, managerial, functional, and organizational capabilities, as well as such things as reputation and history. The investor will be interested in the underlying source of the venture's ability to perform activities either more cheaply, or better, than those of competitors.

Paraphrasing John Kay,[1] a venture's distinctive competence typically arises from

- superior knowledge or a superior ability to respond to changing circumstances;
- unique networks at its disposal;
- a superior reputation (which takes a long time to develop and is difficult to replicate);
- superior R&D ability, prior "wins" in patent races, or both;
- control of strategic assets;
- lower cost structures of incumbent firms; and/or
- exclusivity through market restrictions (such as patents and licensing).

Distinctive competencies and competitive advantages give little more than a temporary advantage, unless they are sustainable over time. Barriers to entry and barriers to imitation can help a venture's competitive advantage remain sustainable. Barriers to entry into the industry may already exist, in which case the investor wants to see that the business possesses a unique entry wedge for getting into the industry. Alternatively, the barriers to entry could be low or nonexistent, in which case the investor wants to see how the new venture, or the environment, is going to erect barriers to entry, barriers to imitation, or both. Of course, it is all the better if both a unique entry wedge is used and further barriers are erected after entry. We now demonstrate how Oceanic Products communicated their distinctiveness to a potential investor.

---

*Oceanic Products' distinctive competence, which will lead to a successful venture, is based on the following foundations:*

*1. **Exclusivity:** There is only one area within Australia that has been infested with hijiki and OCEANIC has been awarded the sole license as a result of their management's prior experi-*

ence in hijiki harvesting, their rapport with the local and state governments, and their Australian citizenship.

2. **Experience:** *Oceanic Products' management has valuable experience in harvesting and processing hijiki; in the crayfish and abalone industries; in commercial diving and the management of commercial divers; in product and service quality management; in project management, budgeting, and finance; in strategy formulation and implementation; and has fluency in the Japanese language and culture.*

3. **Network:** *Oceanic Products' management has strong contacts in the state government's Division of Sea Fisheries and among purchasers both in the domestic and overseas market; Oceanic Products has excellent processing facilities available via an alliance with Goldhammer's fish processing plant; strong contacts and good relationships among the local divers and community and a strong relationship with Asian Foods Inc., the domestic market leader in retailing Asian Foodstuffs, which will allow immediate access to the domestic and overseas markets by utilizing that firm's existing distribution channels.*

4. **Quality:** *The isolated location of the hijiki crop means pollutants are less than 1% of those found in imported hijiki, which are effectively excluded from retail sale by legislation.*

5. **Opposite Season Harvesting:** *Oceanic Products' hijiki will be harvested in the northern hemisphere's "off-season," thus fulfilling the need for fresh, wet hijiki when there is usually limited supply in North Asian markets.*

*In summary, Oceanic Products' competitive advantage arises from their sole license to harvest, their prior experience with hijiki, their contacts and networks, and their ability to supply international markets with a superior product, particularly in the "off-season."*

---

## MARKET ENVIRONMENT
## AND COMPETITOR ANALYSIS

For the investor to develop a positive feel for the opportunity and the new venture, detail about the market is required. A wider perspective of the market often is useful as investors typically will want to know the attractiveness of both domestic and international markets, the segments of those markets, increased detail on the target market and why it was chosen, and detailed analysis of competition within the target market now and in the future.

## INDUSTRY ATTRACTIVENESS

Investors want to assess the attractiveness of the industry and therefore require an industry description and the entrepreneur's assessment of its outlook. Therefore, the business plan must define the industry and assess the attractiveness of the industry today and into the future. To provide this analysis, major trends in the environment need to be identified, made explicit, and justified to the investor. This analysis can begin with the structure of the industry now and compare it with a forecast snapshot of the industry sometime in the future (say, 5 years). The changes in the structural factors of the industry (or strategic area within an industry) over that period of time demonstrate the impact of major trends on industry (or strategic area within an industry) attractiveness. The major issues that need to be addressed are those that influence the

- barriers to entry (to industry, strategic areas, or both) to determine the likelihood of potential new entrants;
- bargaining power of industry members, with suppliers to determine which group is likely to receive which share of profits generated by the industry;
- substitutability of the industry's products with those of another industry, to determine a possible ceiling on the prices of the industry's products;
- bargaining power of industry members with buyers, to determine which group is likely to receive which share of profits generated by the industry; and
- competitive rivalry within the industry, to determine the degree that competitors act to reduce industry profitability.

## OVERALL MARKET AND TARGET SEGMENT(S)

After an assessment of industry attractiveness, investors will attempt to assess the attractiveness of the new venture's position within that industry. This requires information about the market in general, segments of the market and specific details about those segments to be targeted. Information required about the market in general includes the following:

- Size of the current market
- Rate of growth of the market
- Major segments of the market and their characteristics
- Target market, with details on the existing and potential customers within that segment as well as existing and potential competitors serving the target market(s)

In part, windows of opportunity exist because there is not perfect information available, and consequently investors do not expect perfect information to be presented in the plan. But this does not mean they will accept with blind faith all assumptions made, without the support of some evidence or argumentation. Whereas direct information normally is not available, the investor expects that a body of evidence will be produced around the assumptions made, to demonstrate the reasonableness of those assumptions.

This applies particularly to the market research estimates. For example, it is impossible to know what the growth rate of the market is going to be in the future. An assumption of future growth rate then needs to be supported by evidence from other sources, for example, the growth rate for the industry so far, growth rates from comparable industries, and expert opinions as to what the growth rate will be. One by itself is unconvincing to the investor, but the weight of a number of sources helps triangulate and provides validity to the assumption and shows that the management team has done its homework and investigated the business opportunity from many different angles.

The market needs to be segmented in a meaningful way, either through the demographic, geographic, or product-use characteristics of the market, in order that segments of the market can be identified and assessed in terms of attractiveness. The investor is interested in the attractive segment(s) of the market and the critical unsatisfied demands of those segments.

The plan must give the investor a feel for the managers' understanding of "who" are the customers. The plan must indicate the demographic characteristics of potential customers, what their critical needs are, and their ability to pay for those needs. It is important to then investigate those needs in light of how they currently are being satisfied. The plan will need to demonstrate that customers' needs are not being fully satisfied, that is, there is an opportunity to offer a product or service that better meets the needs of the market at a price that customers are willing to pay. The following example comes from the business plan of Breeze Technology:

---

*Nike also is the leader in market segment diversification, having the most comprehensive range of products. Nike is seen as a performance brand first and a fashion statement second. Reebok (with 28% of the market including, their subsidiary Avia), has a fashion and lifestyle image rather than one of performance. Of the minor brands, Keds is the market leader in the children's footwear segment. LA Gear has traditionally produced fashion-oriented products and currently is repositioning itself at the lower priced end of the market. The remaining competitors are aggressively seeking market share through product innovation and marketing campaigns.*

---

Again, from the Breeze business plan:

| The MARKET WANTS | The MARKET GETS | BREEZE OFFERS |
| --- | --- | --- |
| *1. COMFORT* | | |
| Cushioning | Air or gel bags | Improved cushioning |
| Dry feet | Water penetration | Restricted water entry |
| Ventilation | Passive ventilation | Positive moisture evacuation |
| Temperature reduction | Porous fabrics | Positive ventilation |
| Humidity reduction | Holes, vents, sandals | Lower temperatures |
| Odor reduction | Odor Eaters® & other cures Odor prevention | Lower humidity |

## 2. PERFORMANCE

| | | |
|---|---|---|
| Injury avoidance | Structural design | Retains all benefits |
| Rebound or energy return | Air or gel bags | Potential improvements |
| Optimal foot support | Deteriorating foot support as the shoe ages | Optimal foot support for longer period |

## 3. STYLE or FASHION

| | | |
|---|---|---|
| Design Colors Gimmicks Celebrity endorsements | A great variety of designs, color, gimmicks, and celebrity endorsements | Retains all benefits and offers additional possibilities |

## 4. VALUE

| | | |
|---|---|---|
| Price | Price constantly increasing | Insignificant increase in price but significant increase in benefits |
| Benefits | Minimal increase in benefits | |

COMPETITIVE POSITIONING

The plan must demonstrate to investors that the new venture's product offerings will be better positioned in the minds of the customer, relative to competitors' and future competitors' offerings. By *better positioned*, we refer to providing superior value (a higher ratio of quality to price than the competitors) and a more defensible position. This defensible position is in line with the investor's obsession of demanding a sustainable competitive advantage; that is, the new venture's distinctive competence has an excellent match with its external environment that will last even when competitors attempt to imitate. This is the key to convincing investors that this is a viable business opportunity.

*Due to a sole license to harvest the only local source of hijiki, and because future planting is prohibited by strong legislation,*

*Oceanic Products will be highly competitive with hijiki imports in terms of price, quality, and customer service. In the global market, competition comes from Japan, Korea, China, New Zealand, and France. Because the "infestations" in New Zealand and France occur near major ports (seeded by dumped bilge water) they, like the North Asia sources, are relatively high in pollutant content and thus are considered inferior in an increasingly health conscious and affluent North Asian market. The concern with contaminants in foods is a worldwide phenomenon, and as global demand for natural and healthy foods, including highly nutritious seaweed, continues to increase, Oceanic Products' advantage will be extended to world markets.*

The obvious next question in the minds of investors is how are the management team going to position themselves as the high-value provider and in a defensible position? The investor needs to be informed about the decision-making process of customers, the proposed marketing mix, and the firm's growth strategy.

CUSTOMERS' DECISION-MAKING PROCESS

The management team needs to demonstrate their awareness of the ways customers think, and it is from this knowledge that marketing strategy can be directed at those factors that drive the purchase decision and purchase behavior. This could include recognition of the difference between the customer and consumer as well as the difference between primary customer and secondary customer. The customer is the person who buys the product and the consumer is the person who uses or consumes the product, which may or not be the same person. Furthermore, the primary market refers to the group of buyers who directly buy the new venture's products (primary customers), which may then sell to another group of buyers (secondary customers). These differences in both customer or consumer and primary or secondary customers need to be reflected in the marketing strategy.

MARKETING MIX

After demonstrating to the investor an understanding of the minds of the target customers, and the desired location for the new product in the minds of those customers, the plan must detail the concrete action that will be taken to achieve these ends. This involves detailing the marketing mix, that is, the product, price, promotion, and distribution strategies. Whereas each of the marketing mix factors are very important, the investor also is particularly concerned about the cash flow. They want cash coming in the door as soon as is possible (because most new ventures fail as a result of cash flow problems). In the light of that concern, a specific section dedicated toward selling strategies may alleviate some of their concerns.

For example, an investor assessing a new industrial product (that will be used by the customer in the production of another product or service that will be sold again), will have a series of pertinent questions. "Which specific firms are to be targeted? What are the names of the decision makers within those firms? How will they be contacted? When? When will the first sales be made? When will the money come in the door? How long will it take to build up the customer base? How frequently will the customers repeat purchase? What will be the size of orders? Is there any seasonality, and is there anything that can be done to smooth demand? How large is the sales force initially? How fast will the sales force numbers grow? What methods will be employed to motivate salespeople, that is, commission, quota, or bonus?" These details must be provided to potential investors and must also be factored into the financial statements. For example:

---

*Oceanic Products will undertake a comprehensive and proactive marketing strategy. The strategy is based on a joint promotion with Asian Foods Inc., marketing the brand name "Southern Ocean Supreme Hijiki" within Australia and overseas. The cornerstone of the marketing strategy is to gain international recognition of the brand name "Southern Ocean Supreme Hijiki" as a high quality, low contaminant hijiki. The differentiation strategy involves positioning the product in the high quality end of the market using a pull strategy through the distributor. A logo and brand name will be developed to communicate the purity of*

> *"Southern Ocean Supreme Hijiki" and will form the basis of Oceanic Products' future competitive advantage, because the great Southern Ocean stretching down from Australia toward Antarctica is recognized as synonymous with purity and nature.*

---

The business plan needs to detail how the new venture is going to get their products to the market and then how the products or services are going to be promoted to encourage customer trial. Therefore, access to distribution systems and a clear promotion strategy are key investor criteria.

---

> *Distribution initially will be through Asian Foods Inc.—Australia's largest distributor in terms of both sales and turnover. They supply Asian food retailers, health food stores, restaurants, hotels, and airlines. Asian Foods Inc.'s hijiki distribution network in Japan links with the Kerin company, which is estimated to control 60% of the Japanese domestic hijiki market. Asian Foods Inc. also has links with the Arimasu Food Corp.—one of the largest Asian food wholesalers in North America. Asian Foods Inc.'s distribution system can easily absorb Oceanic Products' crop. Oceanic Products has agreed to sell to Asian Foods Inc. the entire first season's harvest at specified prices, assuming quality levels are met. Asian Foods Inc. will achieve a markup on the wholesale price of between 60% to 200%, depending on the product. This underlies Asian Foods Inc.'s desire for a close and continuing relationship with Oceanic Products.*
>
> *The domestic market will use advertising, promotional material, and packaging to emphasize quality, by creating the perception of a healthy product with low levels of pollutants. The marketing also will use the extensive promotion and awareness campaigns carried out by the government and other interest groups, by communicating the positive effects "Southern Ocean Supreme Hijiki" has in achieving community goals. These involve providing employment, developing a globally competitive product, and earning export dollars at the same time fulfilling an*

*environmental purpose through the containment of an introduced weed species.*

---

Investors appreciate an entrepreneur who realizes that "cash is king," that is, the importance of cash flow. Oceanic Products demonstrates an emphasis on cash, by proposing a strategy for reducing accounts receivable and a public relations approach that promotes the company at a minimum cost.

---

*Payment will be based on a 30-day account with a 10% discount on accounts settled within 7 days, which Asian Foods Inc. has agreed to use. These terms provide Oceanic Products with critical cash flow advantages in the early months of production.*

*Oceanic Products will embark on a targeted public relations program that will promote their corporate image throughout the community. Newspaper editorials will promote the image of a local company run by locals, employing locals, restricting the effect of an introduced species and exporting a local product interstate and overseas. The promotion of local events and sporting teams will further integrate Oceanic Products into the hearts and minds of the community.*

---

GROWTH STRATEGY

The marketing strategy must provide evidence to the investor that this new venture has potential to grow (whether through an increase in market share, from overall market growth, or both). But growth also may occur through vertical or horizontal integration, through the development of new products, and by targeting new markets. The growth strategy needs to be detailed to encourage the investors that once again the firm is more than a "one-trick pony" (i.e., not just a company reliant on one product in one market) and that they can be confident they are investing in a high-growth potential business.

Growth requires a strategic deployment of assets in a particular direction. Investors do not want to see the venture growing in all directions at once; they would prefer to see a staged-growth strategy in which growth opportunities are made explicit and pursued in an orderly and possibly sequential fashion (although R&D obviously should be working a few steps ahead). Investors also will be concerned about unsustainable growth rates, when the new venture is growing so fast that it crashes and burns. Growth places considerable strain on resources as well as the management and organization as a whole.

---

For example, James Homes was one of the fastest growing building companies in the early 1990s, riding the crest of the property boom. They grew from two orders for new houses a week in 1990 to 15 houses a week in 1992. The financial and human resources were spread too thin. The quality of houses decreased, they were no longer able to meet deadlines, their inventory and accounts receivable grew disproportionately with sales, and subcontractors were not being paid. James Homes filed for bankruptcy in 1993.[2]

---

Investors are interested in what percentage of the market the management team expects to capture. Assumptions of market share to be gained are often overly optimistic and sometimes quite fanciful, and the investor will keenly assess the realism of such market penetration claims. There is no point in losing credibility with the investor by putting forward wildly optimistic market share claims. Therefore, assumptions of market penetration need to be supported by evidence to provide credibility to the assumption. Growth in market share must be equated to the number of customers and number of individual units sold. This calculation must include not only those customers gained through net increases in market share but also growth of the market.

## RESEARCH AND DEVELOPMENT

The investor will be looking for reassurances that the technology works; that it will be continually improved on; and whether or not there is potential for creating new products, generating new markets that will drive the new venture's growth, or both. The growth engine of the new venture is research and development (R&D). The investor evaluates how the venture is going to maintain its technological lead (if that, it is one of the competitive advantages of the venture).

Therefore, this section of the plan must provide in greater detail the essence of the technology behind the launch product. The investor will want to know "at what stage of development is the technology" for this and other related products, that is, how long before this and other products will be ready for release onto the market. The investor is normally more comfortable if the testing of prototype performance also is performed by a reputable third-party expert.

The investor will be wary of overoptimistic claims in this section of the plan. Claims that many new inventions will emerge miraculously and rapidly from the R&D process (and that each one will be a huge success) will be met with cold skepticism. The difficulty with convincing the investor of future rollout products and markets is that there is little evidence to demonstrate future success with products that are not yet fully through the design phase, not to mention introduced in a future market with unknown demand and unknown competitors. The investor will carefully evaluate the quality of the R&D team, including their experience and track record, and also will assess the amount of resources dedicated to R&D.

The immediate application of R&D should include incrementally improving the existing technology for existing customers. Other sources of growth are through the R&D of new products for existing customers, that make use of existing distribution channels and brand equity. The other method of accomplishing growth is through taking existing products into new markets—that is, sell the existing products in a new geographical region, to a different segment of the market, or come up with new uses for the existing product. Growth also can occur through new products to new markets, usually either through vertical or horizontal integration. The investor will be looking in this section of the plan to be reassured that the management team has a comprehensive growth strategy with rollout products, rollout markets, or both.

Investors want to know what approval process (if any) future products may require from government or regulatory bodies. This will need to include information on the length and cost of the approval process and include an assessment of probability of approval. This is a common consideration for investors in biotechnology ventures.

---

*R&D currently is investigating the use of hijiki in such areas as human and animal nutrition, health products, and medical products. Powdered hijiki concentrate can be formed into tablets for use as a nutritional supplement for human consumption and is being tested as a feed supplement to enhance fitness, stamina, and performance in racehorses. Furthermore, laboratory research is being performed on the anticoagulant properties of hijiki for medical purposes.*

*Oceanic Products also is researching the harvest of sea urchins. A sample shipment to Japan has been well received and negotiations are continuing. The harvesting phase for sea urchins is counterseasonal to that of hijiki. Oceanic Products has been approached by divers from the Japanese companies harvesting sea urchins in Australia, indicating that they would prefer to dive for a company that also can offer them employment harvesting hijiki in the sea urchin "off-season." The possibility of harvesting other types of edible seaweed, in particular kombu, is also being examined.*

---

## MANUFACTURING AND OPERATIONS

The investor does not want the finer details of manufacturing and/or delivery of the service, the position of every machine, how each works and where they will be located. Yet investors do want to know how the manufacturing of the product or delivery of the service will be performed; what, if any, competitive advantages are derived from manufacturing and operations; and an assessment of associated risks and resulting risk reduction strategies to eliminate, or at least reduce, those risks. These investor uncertainties also apply to a predominantly service-based business.

Therefore, this section of the business plan needs to describe how the product will be produced now and in the future. There are various options: for example, self-manufacture, subcontract, or licensed manufacture by an independent business, or a combination of these. Investors also will want to know how many units can be produced under this system and how future growth in sales can be serviced, that is, the means by which capacity will be expanded and when. Investors also are interested in economies of scale and scope and how this equates to different cost levels at different volumes (once again searching for a possible sustainable competitive advantage based on lower-cost superiority). The key here is not to go overboard and provide too much detail. Stick to the one-page budget for this section and include further details, if necessary in the appendices.

Investors constantly search for possible risks to the business. The plan therefore must indicate any critical components to the manufacturing or operations and efforts that have been (or will be) taken to secure those critical components, parts, or suppliers. Issues of lead time, lag time, and quality assurance also should be addressed.

## ORGANIZATIONAL STRUCTURE, MANAGEMENT, AND OWNERSHIP

The investors will want to know how many people need to be employed and the primary duties they will perform, how they will be recruited, compensated, and trained, their position within the organization, and to whom they are answerable. In particular, investors will want to know

- the organizational structure of the business,
- the quality of the management team,
- the complementarity and growth of the management team,
- the legal structure of the business, and
- the ownership structure of the business.

### ORGANIZATIONAL STRUCTURE

A simple organization chart will serve to show each member of the management team's authority and responsibility. Given that the business may grow quickly, two or even three organization charts might be shown, to indicate the changes that are expected to take place in the organizational structure as the business grows. An alternative means of presenting this is to show the initial positions in one color, with phase-two positions in a second color, and so on.

## QUALITY OF THE MANAGEMENT TEAM

The quality of the management team is such an important component of the entrepreneur's communication with the investor that it is addressed in detail in Chapter 4. This section in the business plan is vital to obtaining equity capital, especially from venture capitalists. The investors require details of the management team and their functions within the new venture, including a summary of their qualifications, experience, skills, and knowledge that is related to starting and running the new venture. A full resume for each manager also must be included in the appendixes.

## COMPLEMENTARITY OF THE MANAGEMENT TEAM

The importance of having a complementary team is expressed in Chapter 2. If there is any gap in the management team, investors will need to see the steps outlined by the current management team to secure the right person for the job. This will include specifying the qualifications and experience of the person that will be searched for, as well as how this person will be attracted, for example, a percentage equity set aside for the new manager (with conditions attached). Similar issues may arise as investors think about the planned growth of the business and will wonder when and how the entrepreneurial team will be expanded.

## OWNERSHIP STRUCTURE

This was discussed in detail in Chapter 2. In terms of its clear presentation in the business plan, we suggest that a pie chart is an appropriate means of illustrating who owns what share of the business, prior to the investor's entry into the ranks of equity holders. Another pie chart might be added alongside the first to show the dilution of the existing owners' equities and the share accruing to the investor after the funds are received.

## RISK RECOGNITION
## AND RISK REDUCTION
## STRATEGIES

It would be imprudent not to consider the factors that could threaten the viability of the business. Indeed, the investor will want to see a full understanding of the potential threats that could take away the envisioned strategic competitive advantages. Table 6.2 is a suggested format for conveying to the investor your understanding of potential threats to business profitability and appropriate risk reduction strategies to minimize the likelihood of those threats and/or the impact, if they occur (in the context of the hijiki business).

To expand on the first point of Table 6.2, there is a threat that there will be new discoveries of high-quality hijiki in other locations. Oceanic Products demonstrates that, whereas this is unlikely, they have taken actions to minimize that threat by first securing an exclusive license for the known source of hijiki and then building a reputation in the marketplace as the supplier of quality hijiki. By building a strong market reputation, Oceanic Products is able to establish switching costs that place another company (if another source is discovered) at a competitive disadvantage. Oceanic Products also is continuing to foster its relationship with the local and state governments to not only maintain its exclusive license for their current site but also position itself for a license to any new source of hijiki (if one is ever found).

## FINANCIAL DETAILS

If the investor was excited by the business concept, the window of opportunity, and the entrepreneurial team to manage the venture, this is the section that will heighten the investor's attention. This is where the investor is thinking "what do they want and what's in it for me?" The investor will want to know how much money the new venture will need now and in the future and what that money will be spent on. He or she will want to see what proportion of the money will be raised as equity and what proportion of that money will be raised as debt. He or she will

TABLE 6.2.  Risk Recognition and Risk Reduction Strategies for Oceanic Products

| *Threats* | *Proactive Strategies* | *Reactive Strategies* |
|---|---|---|
| New discoveries of hijiki in other locations | • Secured sole license to harvest and control hijiki infestation<br>• Build reputation for hijiki control<br>• Nurture contacts with other local and state authorities | • Compete vigorously for licenses to control other hijiki outbreaks, on the basis of expertise and successful experience |
| New licenses are issued due to political pressures | • Strong personal relationships built with existing politicians<br>• Use of "natural monopoly" argument | • Sell know-how to other harvesters<br>• Compete vigorously<br>• Consider merger or takeover activity |
| New imports with low pollution levels | • Lobby for more stringent legislation and strong enforcement of existing legislation | • Differentiate on the basis of local origin<br>• Differentiate on the basis of taste, freshness |
| Breakdown in the agreement with Goldhammer's processing plant | • Strong personal relationship built<br>• Contractual agreement signed<br>• Develop plans for own factory | • Build own factory sooner than anticipated<br>• Legal action if necessary to enforce the contract |
| Breakdown in the relationship with Asian Foods Inc. | • Strong personal relationships built<br>• Contractual agreement signed<br>• Keep other distributors "warm" | • Seek other wholesale and retail channels<br>• Export directly to Japan and Korea<br>• Deal direct with major hotels, airlines, restaurants |
| Government increases the royalty rate payable | • Build public support and sympathy<br>• Stay close to the government and argue the inability of the company to sustain a high royalty rate | • Accelerate development of alternative product lines |

want to see the details of the proposed deal, that is, how much capital for a specified amount and type of equity. This section should specify other nonmonetary requirements of the management team on the investor.

The investor will be interested to know the method and timing of a planned harvest and/or exit from the business, that is, when the investor will be able to take out of the business their capital gain. The dividend policy needs to be clearly stated. The return on the investor's funds then can be calculated. Assumptions of discount rates need to be clearly stated. Whereas the investor will no doubt perform his or her own calculations, it is important that rates of return for the investor are stated in the plan to demonstrate the financial feasibility of the business and possibly also as the starting point for negotiations over the equity capital deal. The calculations performed by investors as well as points for negotiation are detailed in Chapter 8.

## SENSITIVITY AND
## SCENARIO ANALYSIS

A sensitivity analysis must be performed to test the robustness of the strategies and the business to variations in the assumptions. The assumptions must be clearly stated. The assumptions must be based on research in the plan. The investor will require that all figures be based on information contained and supported in the body of the plan (see Table 6.3).

TABLE 6.3.  Assumptions Underlying the Scenarios for Oceanic Products

| PRODUCT | VARIABLE | MOST LIKELY SCENARIO | PESSIMISTIC SCENARIO |
|---------|----------|----------------------|----------------------|
| Hijiki | Monthly production rate | 225 tons (wet) | 150 tons (wet) |
|  | Divers' rate | $0.40/kg | $0.45/kg |
|  | Price naturally dried | $28/kg | $18/kg |
|  | Price wet | $5/kg | $3/kg |
|  | Price cut and dried | $38/kg | $35/kg |
|  | Price stems | $5/kg | $1/kg |
| Sea Urchins | Divers' rate | $40/kg | $45/kg |
|  | Sales price | $60/kg | $55/kg |
| Effect on |  |  |  |
| Income | R & D | $62,000 | $62,000 |
|  | Director's fees | $422,000 | $72,000 |
|  | EBIT (first year) | $2,215,443 | $354,534 |
|  | Retained earnings (first year) | $1,375,820 | $199,872 |

---

*The most probable scenario results in a return on investment of 550%. Under a worst-case scenario, this would reduce to 80%. The worst-case scenario, still financially attractive, indicates the financial viability of the business despite adverse circumstances.*

---

FINANCIAL DETAILS

There must be a list of the assumptions underlying the financial tables, even if in a footnote, because the investor's first question will be, "What are these numbers based on?" Better still, list them in a table like Table 6.3, from the business plan of Oceanic Products, and contrast the "most likely" assumptions with those for the "pessimistic" or worst-case scenario. As discussed later in Chapter 8, management should be able to attain at least the "worst-case" scenario results or face charges of incompetence.

Then, in a summary table, show projected sales revenues, *earnings before interest and taxes* (EBIT), *net profit after taxes* (NPAT), and cash balances, for each year over the 5-year horizon. All of this information will be in the detailed pro forma financial statements, but the investor will want to see a summary overview of these results before investigating the financials with a fine-toothed comb.

Also state early in the financial section the *net present value* (NPV) of the business' net cash flows over its 5-year horizon and the *internal rate of return* (IRR), which those cash flows represent. Be sure to reveal the discount rate underlying the NPV calculation. Advice on how to select an appropriate discount rate is provided in Chapter 8.

The pro forma financial statements should include the *profit and loss* (or Income) statements, the balance sheets, and the cash flow statement. These should be prepared at monthly intervals for at least the first year, at quarterly intervals for at least the next 2 years, and also shown on an annual basis for 5 years. Monthly and quarterly cash flow statements are particularly important for the new venture, because they might reveal a dangerously tight cash flow situation or a situation of technical insolvency.

Sensitivity analysis should be performed on a number of key variables, such as price, sales volume, cost of goods sold, and so on, to ensure that the business is not vulnerable to a deviation from the values assumed. In this context, break-even analysis also is recommended, along with a supported argument that the break-even volume is easily attainable.

## THE DEAL—THE ASK AND THE OFFER

State clearly what the business wants from the investor. For example, "How much money? When will it be required and in how many tranches? Are you also looking for access to management advice, the investor's contacts, or both?"

Then, state clearly what the investor is being offered. What share of the equity? Number of seats on the board? Assurances that management will listen to the investor's views, particularly if sales and profit projections are not met. What mechanisms are in place to accede control of the business to the investors if the managers are unable to meet even the worst-case revenue projections?

It is useful to summarize for the investor what rate of return he or she can achieve by accepting your offer. Put this in terms of NPV and return on investment (IRR) and the number of times his or her money will multiply in (say) 5 years. This is your final pitch, so make it a good one! Suggestions for negotiating a deal are detailed in Chapter 8.

## WHAT SHOULD GO IN THE APPENDIXES?

We recommend that you put material in the appendixes that the investor will only want to see if he or she is really interested in investing in your business. Investors rarely read appendixes, because they have lost interest in the business plan at this point or the management team has filled the appendixes with a small mountain of peripheral material.

The appendixes should contain at least the following materials:

- Appendix A: Industry primer—a background paper on the industry, if the audience is broad or the investor is not particularly familiar with your industry (not a good sign)
- Appendix B: Technical material on the new product or service concept
- Appendix C: Resumes of each member of the management team
- Appendix D: Market research survey instrument and results
- Appendix E: Worst-case scenario financial statements

## CONCLUSION

In this chapter, we have been concerned with the presentation of your business via the medium of a formal business plan. If you have done this well, the investor will invite you to come in and make a presentation. So, what makes a compelling business plan? This chapter indicated that the process used is critical to the final output, that is, the task should be iterative and objective. The way the business plan is packaged in terms of clarity and brevity as well as the use of visual aids can have a powerful influence in generating investor excitement about your business.

Nevertheless, all the "sizzle" (the exciting way the information is packaged) in the world will not encourage an investor to part with their money if there is no "steak" (content). This chapter detailed the sections that typically make up a business plan and the appropriate page allocation for each section. Excerpts from business plans supplemented descriptions of the content to be included in each section. The end product should be a business plan that has both "sizzle" and "steak" that generates sufficient investor excitement that you are invited to make a presentation (presentations to a number of different investors, it is hoped). Presenting and defending your business plan in front of investors is the topic of the next chapter.

## NOTES

1. Kay, J. A. (1995). *Foundations of corporate success: How business strategies add value.* New York: Oxford University Press.
2. Names and dates have been changed to protect the identity of this company.

# 7 | Successfully Presenting and Defending Your Business Plan

As detailed in Chapter 5, it is useful to structure your communication process to the investor in a systematic, three-stage process. First (perhaps following a brief telephone conversation about the new venture), the potential investor reads your business plan. Second, if the investor is sufficiently interested, you will be invited to meet with him or her and make a short presentation of yourself and your business concept. Third, this meeting will culminate in a question-and-answer (Q&A) session, when the investor will want to clarify any issues that are not yet clear. In this chapter, we are concerned with the second and third stage—the successful presentation and defense of your business plan.

In Chapter 5 we mentioned that the entrepreneur should look at the three stages as an overall system and plan which topics are to be strategically emphasized in each stage. In the business plan, it is always a good idea to minimize highly technical discussion about how your product works, or the finer details of your service concept, inasmuch as this may be sensitive proprietary information (trade secrets), and once in print it may fall into the wrong hands. Better to save such details for a frank but confidential discussion with the investor during the presentation and Q&A session. Similarly, the finer details of patent protection and registration of brand names and logos simply might be asserted in the plan and covered in more detail in the presentation, Q&A session, or both.

WHAT SHOULD BE PRESENTED?

Although the business plan needs to cover the whole gamut of the business, the presentation need not. If the investor invites you to a meeting after reading the business plan, he or she will be positively inclined toward your business concept but will almost certainly want more detailed information, such as more information on

- the product or service concept,
- your proposed strategy to commercialize the concept,
- the entrepreneurial management team,
- the risks facing the new venture, and
- the financial projections.

Your presentation should address these probable areas of interest and most certainly should not simply reiterate the business plan, page by page. You must presume the investor has indeed read the business plan and would be bored by a simple repetition of the information that is in it. If this assumption is in fact erroneous, the investor will have the opportunity to ask questions in the Q&A period. Better to assume the investor has read the plan, and use the limited time available to best effect by focusing your presentation on the things that the investor probably wants to know more about.

As well as the opportunity to further inform the investor, the presentation and Q&A session are opportunities to persuade the investor of the viability of your business. Investors will want their positive initial reaction to the concept and the management team to be reinforced by a favorable impression of the commitment, enthusiasm, and business acumen of the entrepreneurial team. Doubts remaining in their minds need to be removed by careful anticipation of where those doubts may lie, culminating in a confident presentation of pertinent information and to-the-point answers to questions that arise during the Q&A session.

Investors will not invest in your business if you do not impress them personally. Venture capitalists often say, "We don't invest in products, we invest in people!" During the presentation and the Q&A session, the entrepreneur needs to be aware that the product does not stand on its own: The investors are evaluating the total package.

## THE PRESENTATION TEAM

The people making the presentation to the investor(s) must look and act like a team. How you dress and conduct yourself can present a positive and professional first impression, or oppositely, make the investor(s) uncertain that you are the right person in whom to invest a lot of money. We are not suggesting that you wear a black suit and never crack a smile. Although the presentation is not a funeral, neither is it a picnic (although it may seem to have elements of both!) You need to dress and act appropriately.

### DRESS AND DEMEANOR

What is the appropriate dress? Take your lead from the investors. If they are likely to be wearing business suits, then a suit probably is appropriate (be wary of "casual Fridays"). If they are likely to dress more casually, then you should too. If you are uncertain, err on the more formal side. Slacks (or skirt) and a jacket or blazer over a casual shirt (or blouse) is a safe middle ground. Being too flamboyant in your dress might be taken as a bad sign (unless your business in some way is related to that, such as a fashion house, art studio, or musical group). Although investors are willing to take risks with their money, they need to feel comfortable that they are not entrusting it to someone who has entirely different precepts about what is, or is not, appropriate business behavior.

Of course, dress conventions constantly are evolving, and differ from city to city within nations, not to mention between nations. They differ between industries as well, with the information technology industry being notable for its impact on introducing more casual dress conventions into the workplace. Similarly, it may be a defining characteristic of entrepreneurial men that they are allergic to neckties, so there is little point wearing a tie if it makes you awkward, uncomfortable, and unable to present yourself in the best possible way.

Personal grooming is important, of course, in giving a good impression. It goes without saying that you need to be neat and clean, even if you have just come from the lab or the workshop. A recent haircut to trim those wayward locks (if you are fortunate enough to have any) also is a good idea.

Finally, entrepreneurial teams need to look like teams. Although we do not advocate wearing uniforms or identical suits or outfits (unless this is part of the presentation to demonstrate the appearance of the people working in the business), some semblance of cohesion among the team members probably is desirable. Just imagine one member in a suit (all neatly cropped), another in T-shirt and shorts, with unruly hair (apparently fresh from a day at the beach), and a third member in holed blue jeans and scruffy jacket. Does this look like a team of people who can work together and agree on anything? Perhaps they can, but first impressions count for so much, and you do not want your major obstacle to be the investor's unspoken concern that "these guys don't look like a very cohesive team."

So, if two or more members of the entrepreneurial team are making a presentation to an investor, take a moment to coordinate your outfits. Decide that you all will wear suits, or all wear casual shirts and jackets, for example. If suits, decide to wear darker suits rather than lighter suits. We have heard venture capitalists express a preference for darker suits over lighter suits, making unfavorable comparisons with car salespersons! We also have heard the comment on another occasion that, "If they want to be treated like businessmen they should look like businessmen!" The same surely goes for businesswomen.

Now, concerning demeanor. Be earnest but with the occasional lighter moment. Humor is a wonderful additive. When people laugh, they listen harder, just in case you might be funny again! But your job is not to entertain; it is to inform and persuade, so do not overdo it. Address the investor directly: Do not speak to the back of the room or to others in the room who are not involved in the decision to be made. Make and keep eye contact with each of the investors, without staring them down, of course. Don't be too aggressive. Don't speak too loudly. Gestures such as stabbing your finger (pointing) toward the investor are usually poorly received. Don't violate the unspoken laws of physical proximity—many investors will feel very uncomfortable if you are "in their face."

Do not patronize the investor. Don't explain things in detail that you should reasonably expect the investor to fully understand already. If he or she does not understand, a question probably will arise later. You must be careful not to make any comment that might alienate one or more of the investors present. You want their support, not their animosity.

WHO SHOULD PARTICIPATE?

The investor(s) will not want to be looking across the table at 5 or 10 members of the entrepreneurial team. Only the top decision makers in the entrepreneurial team should be involved in the presentation. There is sometimes a case for other key personnel also presenting, such as a scientist or engineer who may be the main repository of the intellectual property and who can best answer the more technical questions that arise. All members of the top management team must be present (even though not all will be involved in the presentation). Investors invest in people, and they will want to form their impressions about the competency of each manager and the cohesiveness of the managerial team during the Q&A session.

## A SUGGESTED PLAN FOR
## THE PRESENTATION

Carefully plan your presentation. Do not expect to "just stand up and tell them about it." Under pressure, you may forget things you wanted to say or repeat yourself excessively. You may also talk too long, and the investor's time (and patience) will be limited. Plan for the presentation to take only 20 minutes. Assuming the investor has allocated you an hour of his or her time, there should be ample time for questions and answers.

Next, decide what you want to accomplish in that 20 minutes, and set a "time budget" that uses that 20 minutes to maximum advantage. In Table 7.1 we suggest the main components of your presentation and the time that should be allocated to each.

Note that this presentation effectively is divided into three main parts: about one third on the product, service, or business concept (sections one and two); about one third on the management team (sections three, four, and five); and about one third on financial matters (sections six and seven). That is, the strategic analysis, the risks recognized, and the risk reduction strategies will reflect strongly on the skills and competence of the management team.

Remember that you should have strategically decided to leave out some of the finer details: The investor always can ask a question to clarify an issue after the presentation. For example, in the presentation you may make reference to your product and its web of intellectual property protection, strategically leaving out the details regarding the status of patents, trademarks, and registered brand names but being ready to provide those details when asked. Also, you might decide to minimize discussion of a particular issue in the presentation (such as patent protection), because you foresee no problems in that area and are very confident about your ability to answer questions. Conversely, you may wish to avoid questions in a particular area (for example scientific issues, if you do not bring your chief scientist with you) and consequently want to cover those aspects more thoroughly in the presentation, perhaps using video, computer animation, or both.

WHO SHOULD DO THE TALKING?

We believe the CEO typically should open and close the presentation, so he or she should take sections one and seven at least. But inasmuch as the investors particularly will want to evaluate the CEO, he or she should proceed through sections two and three until it is time for another team member to extol the CEO's virtues. That next speaker usually would be the chief marketing officer, who should continue through section four, until introducing the chief operations officer to talk about operations, R&D, and the human resources plan, before introducing the chief financial officer who must present section six. Finally, the CEO will stand up again to summarize and present the deal.

It is usually not necessary that everyone present speak during the presentation. Some might be there in case of highly technical questions. No more than four people should speak in any 20-minute presentation, inasmuch as that tends to make the presentation too disjointed. Transitions from one speaker to the other should be nearly seamless. All members will have been introduced at the start of the presentation, so each speaker can finish on a strong point and simply move back to his or her chair, as the next speaker simply stands and announces his or her purpose (for example, "I will now present our strategic plan"). Alternatively, the person finishing his or her section might provide a transition, such as, "Bob will now take you through the financials."

TABLE 7.1.  Suggested Outline and Time Budget for the Presentation

---

**1. Introduction:**                                                  1-2 minutes
- Identify each of your team members, and their titles.
- We represent (business name), which is in the business of (define business field) and our mission is to (mission statement).
- Overview what your product or service is or does.
- State your purpose today (to introduce you to our business and seek $X funding).

---

**2. Your product, service, and business concept:**                   5-6 minutes
- What is the problem you solve—the market need to be satisfied. How do you know this?
- Details of your product or service—how it works, how it creates customer satisfaction.
- Stage of the technology—prototypes, alpha and beta site tests, orders, sales?
- Market support for your product—sales so far, market research results?
- Testimonials—from credible buyers, preferably accompanied by orders.

---

**3. Your management team:**                                          2-3 minutes
- It's a great product or service concept, and we have a strong team to bring it to market.
- CEO details the qualifications and credentials, and relevant experience of the others.
- Show that the functional skills of the team members are complementary to each other.
- Another member details the qualifications, experience, & leadership skills of the CEO.

---

**4. Your strategic plan:**                                           3-5 minutes
- Analysis of the competitive environment, including potential rivals
- Strengths, weaknesses, opportunities, and threats for all players
- Your strategic options, the one chosen, and why
- The marketing plan—product design choice, price, promotion, distribution, warranty
- The sales plan—including extensions into new regions
- The operations plan—including production and transportation logistics
- The R&D plan—including expected dates for product upgrades and new products
- The human resources plan—including growth, training programs, incentives

---

## GET THE INVESTOR EXCITED ABOUT
## YOUR PRODUCT OR SERVICE CONCEPT

As mentioned earlier, in most cases approximately the first third of the presentation should be devoted to a demonstration of the product, service, or business concept. Most readers will finish reading your business plan and be left with some questions about exactly how your

TABLE 7.1. Continued

| 5. **Risk and risk reduction strategies:** | 1-2 minutes |
| --- | --- |

- What do you perceive as the major risks facing your business?
- What are your proactive risk mitigation strategies?
- What are your reactive recovery strategies if those risks materialize?

| 6. **The financial projections:** | 4-5 minutes |
| --- | --- |

- Summary bar charts—sales, profit, and cash balances for each of the first 5 years
- Pie charts indicating revenue from different product lines, geographic areas, or both
- Net present value of cash flows plus the "end-of-horizon" valuation of the business
- Internal rate of return generated by the business over the 5-year horizon
- Brief reference to the worst-case scenario, lines of credit available if needed, and so forth
- Refer briefly back to risk reduction strategies and confidence in the expected case

| 7. **Summary and the deal:** | 1-2 minutes |
| --- | --- |

- We have demonstrated the quality of our business concept, our management team, our strategic plan, and the financial viability of our business.
- The ask—We are seeking $X to fund establishment expenses, working capital needs for the first X months, intellectual property protection, and ongoing R&D activity.
- The offer—For that $X, we offer XX% of the equity in our company, X seats on the board, and an internal rate of return on your investment of X% over 5 years, which equates to X times your money back in 5 years.
- Thank you for your attention, and we look forward to responding to your questions.

product works or exactly how your service concept differs from others. This is the first hurdle you need to overcome. Investors need to be convinced that the product or service concept is workable and commercially viable before they will consider investing in you or your company.

MULTIMEDIA PRESENTATION

In the presentation, you also should use other media (such as audio, video, and computer animation) as they are more powerful at communicating the business concept and viability than the stated or printed word supplemented with basic charts and figures. Moving images that demonstrate how your product or service concept actually works are worth 1,000 words. Moving images of a working prototype are more convincing than detailed drawings or inanimate models. Seeing it used in different ways by different people is more compelling than several paragraphs asserting that the concept is widely applicable.

Thus, a videotape demonstrating the product or service in operation may be the best means of supporting claims made in the business plan. But don't be too fancy—this is not Hollywood. Background music (if any) must be chosen carefully and must complement rather than intrude on or detract from the presentation. Do not dwell too long on images or scenes. Get the message over, then move on to the next point. Investors can be an impatient lot, and they are smart enough to absorb things quite quickly! The video need only be 2 or 3 minutes in duration.

Communication of ideas usually is more effective if the information is transmitted and received in two or more mutually reinforcing ways. Support your verbal presentation with a video backup, overhead slides showing the bullet points, or a series of still photographs that serve to illustrate a series of points you are making. This will serve to more firmly fix the ideas in the audience's mind. These are now discussed in greater detail.

### Overhead Slides

There is an art to using overhead slides. You must not repeat word-for-word the words that are on the slide. This drives people crazy, particularly if they have watched a lot of presentations and know the difference between a good presentation and a bad one. Use different words that mean the same thing. Do not have too much information on a slide, and say more than is written on the slide. Bullet points are a summary of the points you are making, not the entire story. Do not try to cram too much onto each slide or make the writing too small. More than 10 lines look very crowded and busy. Use a font size of at least 48 for headings, 40 or 44 for main points, and 36 or 40 for indented (secondary) points. Third-level bullet points (at a font size of, say, 32) should be used sparingly, inasmuch as they make the slide look especially busy. Whatever you do, do not put up slides that are simply copied from printed pages (12 font) in the business plan or other documents. This is the antithesis of communication!

The "PowerPoint" program in Microsoft "Office Internet Assistants" is an ideal slide presentation package, which either can be printed out on acetate slides as shown directly on a computer screen or projected onto a screen via a Barco or other computer projection system. PowerPoint, or other presentation software (in packages such as Claris Works), allows

**TABLE 7.2.** Suggested Layout for a PowerPoint Slide

Presentation to Investor Corp. ——————————

## Window of Opportunity

- Increase in Asians visiting Australia
- Tough legislation against pollutants
- Legislation prevent further infestation
- Increased demand for health & natural foods
- Public support for "green" companies

Oceanic Products © 1998

you to use color, insert photographs, graphics, charts, and a variety of other effects (including sounds) that can make your presentation more effective.

Use color wisely. Reds and oranges do not show up well, particularly in rooms that are not completely dark. White or yellow lettering on a dark background (such as royal blue) is recommended. Black lettering on a clear background usually is considered old fashioned and passé. Jazz it up a little, for better visual impact. Add colored lines or boxes. Use PowerPoint's "build" feature to build up a slide, one bullet point at a time. Use another feature to have the new bullet point slide in from the right, for example. But do not overdo it. Too much clutter, or too many visual gimmicks, can negatively affect the credibility of your presentation. Table 7.2 shows an overhead slide (produced using Microsoft PowerPoint) similar to that used by Oceanic Products in a presentation to potential to investors.

For the PowerPoint slide, the background is navy blue, borders are red (including "Presentation to Investor Corp." and "Oceanic Products © 1998), heading (Window of Opportunity) is yellow and the text in bullet points is white.

Similarly, go easy on the use of sounds to accompany your PowerPoint slides. That program allows you to herald each new bullet point with one or another sound, such as a car smash, or applause, whooshing noises, or many other wild and wonderful sounds. Use these very sparingly, if at all, as they tend to distract the listener, in our view, and thereby detract from your presentation. Repetitive use of the same sound can be boring and worse still, annoying.

Given the speed and memory capacity of personal computers today, the entire presentation might be made from the hard disk of a laptop computer, rather than switching between VCR and slide projector. Multimedia presentations allow video inserts to be presented, as well as text overlay on a video (moving) backdrop, which can be very effective. Such text might be the names and titles of a person speaking on the video, excerpts or quotes from what they are saying, or bullet points that parallel your verbal presentation.

## CONVINCE THE INVESTOR THAT
## THE MANAGEMENT TEAM ADDS VALUE

As mentioned previously, investors need to be convinced that the management team adds value over and above the new venture's product offerings. This task, in part, involves outlining how the team will manage the commercialization of the opportunity, including marketing, production, and research and development. It also includes convincing the potential investor that this company is not a "one-trick pony" and that the management team has the skills to roll out future products.

In this part of the presentation, you need to communicate two main things: first, the qualifications and experience of the management team and, second, the selected strategies and implementation tactics. (Alternatively, you may prefer to cover the strategic plan first, then show that the managers are capable of implementing the plan as a follow-on to the human resources plan.) In the plan, you will have outlined the various strategic options open to you and chosen one. In the presentation, you might briefly list these again, or simply state the option chosen and defend its choice in terms of the opportunities presented and the constraints imposed by the market environment and by competitors' actions, potential reactions, or both.

Give considerable detail about your marketing mix and sales plan. Outline where and how you plan to reach the potential customer. Finer details here can be very impressive and should serve to convince the investor that you have thought the process all the way through, to the point of purchase and beyond to warranty and repair service. Similarly, your operations plan, your R&D plan, and your human resources development plan, deserve more detailed analysis, to clarify what you have said briefly in the business plan and to demonstrate that you have thought things all the way through.

An area of major importance is risk recognition and risk reduction strategies. The investor will almost certainly ask you, "What do you think are the major risks facing your business?" unless you address it in the presentation. Better to be prepared for this and address it in your presentation in a planned way, rather than "shoot from the hip" when the question arises. List all the risks you consider important, and show (with appropriate audio-visual backup) what strategies you have proactively put in place to mitigate each risk. Admit that you may not be able to avoid the risks entirely, and show your reactive strategies as well, that is, what you would do if the problem did in fact arise.

Presentation of these items will give a good impression of the management team, their business acumen, and their familiarity with all aspects of the business. Follow this with a short account of each person's educational qualifications and relevant work experience (especially start-up experience) for the role they are to play in the new venture. Stress the complementarity of the team members by emphasizing their different backgrounds, experiences, and/or qualifications, and at the same time demonstrate that all members of management can work together as a team. The investors will make an assessment of the management team based on what is said and also the way the business plan, presentation, and Q&A session are approached.

## COMMUNICATE THE FINANCIAL
## VIABILITY OF THE NEW VENTURE

The final third of the presentation assumes that the first two thirds have generated enthusiasm in the product and business concept and trust and respect for the management team. The final main task is to communicate the financial viability of the new venture and the robustness of the financial forecasts. If done well, this will reinforce the impressions gained on the first two issues.

The investor will have examined the pro forma financial statements carefully, if he or she is interested in your business concept, so what is

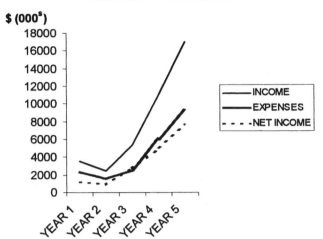

**Figure 7.1.** Sample Graph of Financial Performance

needed in the presentation is a summary overview, not myriad details. Questions on finer details can be asked in the Q&A session and will allow the investors to really focus the spotlight on the area of their concern. Whereas the business plan will make extensive use of columns and rows of numbers to present the financials (with some graphs, pie charts, and bar charts of course), the presentation of the financials should be almost entirely graphs and charts. Showing pictorially the growth of sales over time, or the proportion of revenues going to various expense categories, and so on, can have a much greater impact than simply words, words, and more words. A simple example is demonstrated in Figure 7.1.

Make sure you mention the net present value of the business, explicitly noting the discount rate used and the internal rate of which the business concept is expected to achieve.[1]

## PITCH THE DEAL AND BEGIN
## THE NEGOTIATION PROCESS

Now it is time for "the ask and the offer." You want to raise $X million. That is the "ask." In return for those funds, you will offer X% of the equity in the business, one or more seats on the board, and so on.

Take a few moments to justify the offer. The X% is based on the net present value of the business being $Y million and the funding provided (say, $F) being X% of that net present value. (i.e., $F/Y = X\%$). Note that the investor's $F effectively will be compounding at Z% (the internal rate of return) over the investment period, and at the specified time horizon the investor could sell his or her stock for $XX million, which is N times his or her initial investment! This is essentially your opening claim, and the negotiation process will continue from this point. (These concepts and the negotiating process are the subject of Chapter 8.)

Finally, at about the 20-minute mark of your presentation, you thank the potential investors for their attention and express your willingness to answer any questions they might have.

## THE Q&A SESSION

The written business plan (stage I) and the presentation (stage II) gives the entrepreneur the opportunity to communicate the viability of the new venture and the investment opportunity. The question and answer (Q&A) session (stage III) is the opportunity for the investor to delve deeper into the business and to look for possible fatal flaws, unrealistic assumptions, and/or points of leverage for negotiating a better deal. Conversely, the Q&A session provides the entrepreneur the opportunity to remove any lingering doubts that an investor may have. A potential investor with lingering doubts, whether expressed or silent, will mean that no money will change hands.

The Q&A session can be a challenging and stressful time for the entrepreneur. Preparation is the best defense. We suggest that the following basic rules be followed:

### ANSWER THE QUESTION ASKED

Too often the entrepreneur goes off at a tangent with a vast explanation of something that is an answer to a question the investor did not ask and leaves largely unanswered the specific question that was asked. The investor might attempt to redirect the question one more time but may decide that you did not understand the question, and by extension, do not fully understand your business. If you are uncertain about the question, it is surely better to clarify the question before answering it, such as "Let me see if I fully understand your question. Are you asking whether or not we have considered . . . "

The entrepreneur (or the entrepreneurial team) needs to listen very carefully to each question. Most people find it a good idea, particularly when the question is really a series of related questions, to jot down in shorthand form the questions as they are asked. It is all too easy to forget the third and fourth parts of a question after going into too much detail in the first two parts. Giving concise and pertinent answers to all four parts of the question in succession makes you look very competent.

## TREAT ALL QUESTIONS WITH RESPECT

There are phrases we can say off handedly in our daily lives that can be disastrous in a Q&A session. For example, the phrase "That's a very good question!" should not be used as a preface to addressing the question. The investor would not have asked the question if he or she thought it was a dumb question! Saying "That's a good question" also may be taken to imply that other questions were not so good. It also implies that you are the supreme expert and judge of what is a good question, whereas the investor often will have a great deal of experience in the industry concerned and may feel that he or she is a better judge of the merit of a question.

Treat all questions with respect, even if the answer is in the business plan and the investor apparently has forgotten reading it (or merely skimmed through your plan). If this happens, say something like "In the business plan, on page 8, we address that issue, but I would like to emphasize the following . . . " An embarrassed investor is probably an alienated investor.

## BREVITY IS A VIRTUE

You know a lot about your business. But the investor has a simple question (or perhaps a more complex question or series of questions) on the table right now and has potentially 20 other questions that he or she would like to ask if there is time available. If those other questions are not asked, he or she may go away with remaining doubts about your product, your strategy, or your ability to manage the business. It is imperative to let all questions be aired, to remove all doubts, and, it is hoped, leave the investor satisfied with your answers.

So be brief and to the point. Do not waste the investor's time with long and roundabout answers, illustrative examples, or other stories. Carefully ascertain what the investor wants to know, and give him or her the quintessential answer to that question as concisely as possible. Then stop talking. Let the investor ask a follow-up question, if he or she wants finer details about that issue. Do not wax eloquently about all the finer details at first, inasmuch as the investor simply might be testing your knowledge about the general issue. You might say, "The short answer to that is . . . " and conclude this answer by saying "I can go into more detail if you would like me to."

When the investor says "I have no more questions," this can signal one of two things; either (a) I have made up my mind to invest or (b) I have made up my mind to not invest. A subset of the latter includes (c) it is not worth asking any more questions because the entrepreneur does not have the answers or does not understand the question.

RESPONSIBILITY FOR PARTICULAR QUESTIONS

When an entrepreneurial team makes a presentation to an investor, each member present should have a defined managerial or key operating role in the new business, such as chief executive officer (CEO), chief marketing officer (CMO), chief financial officer (CFO), chief operations officer (COO), chief scientist, and so on. The investor will want to evaluate each of the managers in the context of the role they will play in the new venture. Thus, they will want to hear the CMO answer questions on the marketing strategy, not the CFO or the COO. Similarly, the CFO is the person with responsibility for the financial details presented, should answer most questions in that area, and so on.

Why do we say *most* questions and not *all* questions concerning the financials? The CEO needs to be "on top of it all" and demonstrate his or her understanding of all aspects of the business and should take the lead and answer those finance (or marketing, operations, research and development, etc.) questions that relate to the new venture's overall competitive strategy. Couching the answer in terms of the firm's mission and its chosen competitive strategy also tends to impress investors, if not too repetitive.

LET THE LEADER LEAD

The investor will pay most attention to the leader of the entrepreneurial team, the CEO. The CEO is the person who will need to exercise leadership, direct the activities of the others, and remove them from management roles if necessary. If the investor becomes dissatisfied about any facet of the business, and wants to enforce a change, it is the CEO to whom he or she will talk. It follows that the investor will want to see the CEO exhibit leadership qualities and that this leadership is recognized and accepted by the other members of the entrepreneurial team.

So, let the leader exhibit his or her leadership skills! If a question is put to the team in general, rather than to a specific member, the others should "hold their fire" and let the CEO answer it. Even when it is clearly a marketing question (for example) the CEO might say, "Let me make a general comment on that before handing it over to my chief marketing officer for more detail." In this way, the leader asserts his or her leadership and the other members are seen to recognize and accept it. Similarly, if a question is asked of a particular member (say the CFO) but is really a corporate strategy issue, the CFO should say something like, "I could offer you our firm's view on that, but inasmuch as it is a strategy issue, I defer to the CEO, who ultimately is responsible for such decisions."

DON'T "ADD ON" TO A TEAM MEMBER'S ANSWER

Although it is extremely tempting, resist the temptation to add a further comment to another team member's answer. "Let me add to that . . . " is the bane of the investor who already has received a sufficient answer to the question asked and wants to move on to another issue. Such add-ons almost inevitably are repetitive and usually add little of value, given their opportunity cost (namely an answer to the investor's next question). A second and a third "add-on" from other team members almost certainly will alienate the investor. Following what we said about brevity earlier, it follows that there is more that could be said in response to the question but that the person answering it has chosen to not say, awaiting a follow-on question if the investor does indeed want more detail.

There are two main exceptions to this rule. The first is when the answer given by a team member is wrong, at variance with the facts or data presented in the business plan. Here the CEO should politely override the other manager and say something like, "That's not quite right. What we have decided to do is to . . . " If the CEO makes the mistake, and the question relates to the finances, for example, the CFO would politely add in something like, "That's not quite right. I am responsible for the finer details of the financials and can tell you that the rate we have assumed is . . . "

The second main exception to the no add-on rule is when the respondent has missed the point of the question, has gone off on a tangent, or both. Again the CEO (or the appropriate functional expert) should intervene with something like, "I think the question related more to . . . " and attempt to get the answer back on track. This exception also applies when the person responding to the question is momentarily confused, or suffers from stage fright, and cannot remember the main points of a prerehearsed answer to that particular question.

## COMMON QUESTIONS YOU MAY BE ASKED

We now provide a list of common questions asked by investors and suggest a format for answering these questions. If you have spent some time thinking through the answers to these questions, in the context of your new business, you will be in a much better position to answer them well (under what may well be fairly stressful conditions). Strong answers to these questions will give the impression that you have given a lot of thought to every aspect of your business plan. Answers that seem to roll effortlessly off the tongue (but which were in fact rehearsed) give the investor great confidence that you understand your business and are capable of managing it (and the investor's money!). This is not creating a false impression for the investor; the fact that you correctly guessed the questions and had prepared appropriate answers does indicate professionalism.

We are strong advocates of trying to anticipate all the questions that the investors will ask, and consider it a triumph when a team only receives questions that were anticipated. This requires long and careful thought by each member of the presentation team and several intensive practice Q&A sessions with someone playing the "devil's advocate" and asking hard questions, ignorant questions, even off-the-wall crazy questions, because sometimes that is exactly what investors will do. Many of the questions will relate, directly or indirectly, to risks, risk recognition, and risk reduction strategies. You must think through all the things that could possibly go wrong and what you would do if they did go wrong. (Murphy's Law is alive and well in entrepreneurship!)

It is an excellent practice to write down all the questions you can anticipate and then formulate a perfect answer to each one. Write down each answer to each question, and print out the entire Q&A list for bedtime reading for all members of the management team. Although the CMO is primarily responsible for the marketing questions, and so on for the COO and CFO, each member of the team should know the "company view" on each issue. This can be of great value if the CMO (for example) stumbles in answering a detailed marketing question, because another team member, preferably the CEO, can come to the rescue. This cross-discipline knowledge also enhances consistency and the impression of team cohesion.

## QUESTIONS ON PROPRIETARY INTELLECTUAL PROPERTY AND ITS PROTECTION

- What do you actually own that is not available to an existing or a potential rival firm?
- How will you protect your service or business concept from imitation by new competitors?
- At what stage in the patent application process are you?
- What exactly is patentable about your product or process? How many "claims" have you made and what, specifically, are they?
- How long will it take for someone to invent around your patent?
- How long do you think it will take before rival products enter the market and compete?
- What will you do then? What strategies will you have in place to counter this?
- What overseas patent applications have you filed, or do you plan to file?
- What if your patent application fails?
- Have your registered your company name, brand names, logos yet? In what jurisdictions?
- Is a patent worth any more than the paper it is written on? Can you afford to defend your patent?

## QUESTIONS ON YOUR MARKET, TARGET CUSTOMER, AND MARKET RESEARCH

- Who is your typical target customer; what does he or she do?
- You have listed customer benefits accruing from product ownership, but which are the most important?
- Which of these benefits will you emphasize in your advertising and promotional activity? Will this vary for different market segments?
- How or where does your target customer actually buy the product?
- Sure it's a better product, but how do you know that people will actually buy it?
- Tell me more about your market research? Was any of it formal and scientific?
- I do not see a copy of the questionnaire in the appendixes—what questions did you ask?
- Where are the tabulated results of your market research? Are they statistically significant?

## QUESTIONS ON YOUR MARKETING STRATEGY

- Please explain your choice of price, quality positioning for your product, or both.
- What distribution channels will you use? How will you gain access to them?
- What is your advertising and promotion strategy?
- How will you push sales? What is the reward structure for sales personnel? Why?
- Where and when will your production take place? why there? why not closer to your main customers?
- How do you plan to get the product to the customer? Explain the logistics and transportation details.
- What customs duty classification does your product fall under?
- What is your R&D plan? What are you currently working on? What is the anticipated rollout plan for new products?
- What is your human resources plan? training programs? Is there upward mobility for people within your organization, or must they leave you to get ahead?
- What incentive systems do you have in place to ensure employee loyalty and ongoing productivity improvement?

## QUESTIONS ON YOUR SUSTAINABLE
## COMPETITIVE ADVANTAGES

- Couldn't a new firm set up production and steal half your market if and when you demonstrate that there is indeed a market for this product or service?
- Which of the competitive advantages you cite are more than "first-mover" advantages and are likely to endure? for how long?
- We've heard all about your first-mover advantages. What first-mover disadvantages do you foresee?

## QUESTIONS ON YOUR FINANCIAL PROJECTIONS

- Suppose I cut your sales projections by 20% and raised your cost estimates by 15%, would you break even? (or, what would this do to your NPV and IRR figures?)
- You have discounted your cash flows by X%, which I regard as way too low. What would happen if we discount them by 50%?
- You have used a price/earnings ratio of X. What is your basis for that particular PE ratio?
- What is your worst-case scenario? I mean, what assumptions are you making for that scenario?
- Your gross margin is only X%. After rivals emerge, almost certainly there will be vigorous price competition. How far do you think prices will fall, and do you think you can survive an extended price war?

## QUESTIONS ON THE DEAL

- You want me to put up $X million and yet you are only offering me Y% of the equity. For that kind of money, I want more than 50% of the equity. Can we make a deal?
- What assurances can you give me that I can get my money out if things go wrong?
- I'll settle for a minority equity share if I can have a majority of the seats on the board of directors, so I can bring in new managers if things do not work out the way you say they will. What do you say?

## CONCLUSION

In this chapter, we have addressed the second and third stages of the communication process, the presentation, and the Q&A session. This chapter details the importance of strategically deciding which information about the business should be included in the presentation and which information should be left out of the presentation, with the expectation that a question will be asked. An average presentation merely informs an investor, whereas a good presentation informs and persuades the investor of the business's viability. This chapter provided a number of helpful hints for persuading investors that include the selection and coordination of the presentation team, their dress and demeanor, and their management of presentation time.

The chapter further detailed techniques that could be used to generate investor excitement about a business. Once excited, an investor needs to be persuaded that the management team has the capability of successfully navigating the business. Therefore, the presentation must communicate the qualifications and experience of the management team, the selected strategies and implementation tactics, and the financial viability of the business. The presentation concludes with the "ask" and the "offer" and an invitation for questions.

The Q&A session is an opportunity for the investor to delve deeper into the business and at the same time is an opportunity for the management team to remove any lingering doubts the investor(s) may have. This chapter proposed a number of rules the management team can follow to improve their performance in the Q&A session. Underlying all of these rules is the notion that preparation is the best defense. The chapter also provides a list of common questions asked by investors and suggests a format for answering these questions.

If the business plan, presentation, and Q&A session have been successful, the investor will want to negotiate a deal. Key to negotiating a deal is the value of the business. Valuing the business and negotiating the deal are addressed in the next chapter.

## NOTE

1. The next chapter provides more detail on net present value, discount rate, and internal rate of return.

# 8 | Valuing the Business and Negotiating the Deal

In this chapter, we consider the valuation of the business and, consequently, what the investor's money is worth in terms of equity in the business. We also address the issue of how to negotiate a better deal with the investor, given that the investor is almost certain to want a larger share of the business (for any given cash infusion) than the entrepreneur wants to give. The investor also may want a position of ultimate control, either initially via a majority shareholding or ultimately via clauses that allow control to revert to the investor if the management team does not achieve specific targets relating to sales, profits, or other objectives.

The entrepreneur must know what the business is worth and be able to explain his or her valuation as the outcome of a series of underlying assumptions and subsequent calculations. Any disagreement on the valuation then can be focused on a disagreement on one or more of the underlying assumptions, and agreement or compromises on the valuation (and hence the share going to the investor) can be negotiated. The valuation of the business rests on assumptions underlying the following six issues:

- The discount rate applied to future revenues and costs
- Sales revenue (i.e., sales volume at the stated prices) in each period considered
- Costs of goods sold and operating expenses
- Accounting conventions and processes used (e.g., depreciation method)

- The number of periods considered (i.e., the time horizon chosen)
- The price-earnings multiple applied to the "end-of-horizon" profits

We shall discuss these six major assumptions that determine the value of the business in detail in this chapter. But in addition, we note that the share of the business going to the investor depends on the timing and type of cash infusions. In general, if all the funds are not required "up-front," it is cheaper, in terms of share of the business given away, to take the cash in stages. It is cheaper (in terms of equity given away) to stage the infusion of funds as the value that the business should grow to over time and the risk decrease, such that a given dollar amount invested will be worth a lesser share of a more valuable and less risky business.

In terms of the type of cash received, we must consider the issue of debt versus equity. Most new ventures have insufficient collateral or cash flow to attract debt funding early in their existence. As the new venture matures, debt funding becomes increasingly attractive, as it allows the entrepreneur to retain his or her equity share (and the dividend income and capital gains that follow) without causing undue financial distress on the new venture.[1] Hybrid funding, such as *convertible debt* (i.e., debt that can be converted to equity at a specified period of time or the failure to meet specified performance levels), also should be considered, depending on the new venture's circumstances.

## THE VALUATION OF THE BUSINESS

Let us assume for the moment that the investor will agree that all the cash flows presented in the new venture's financial statements are correct (or best estimates). Now, how do we properly value those cash flows? We cannot simply add year one net cash flows to year two net cash flows, and so on, because a dollar received this year is worth more than a dollar earned next year. After all, a dollar received this year can be deposited in a bank and earn interest such that it grows to more than a dollar by year two. We need to consider how much interest each dollar held can earn while we are waiting for the net cash flows of later years to arrive.

NET PRESENT VALUE ANALYSIS

*Net present value* (NPV) analysis, also known as *discounted cash flow* (DCF) analysis, is used to "discount" future cash flows back to their present value so that we can add them to current (present) period net cash flows (which already are expressed in their "present value" because they are received or disbursed in the present period). Future cash flows are discounted back to a lesser amount of "present value" dollars, because that lesser amount could grow to a larger amount in the future if it were held in the present period. For example, if I had 91 cents today, it would grow to about $1 in a year if I could obtain 10% interest on that 91 cents (i.e., .91 + .091 = 1.001). Thus, a dollar to be received in a year's time should be valued at no more than 91 cents today, if I can earn 10% on any funds that I hold today.

We assume that most readers will be familiar with NPV or DCF analysis, so we will not attempt to teach it here. The above example should suffice to show that future cash flows must be discounted by the appropriate interest rate, which is, naturally, known as the *discount* rate. Cash flows from years two, three, four, five, and further into the future must be discounted more heavily, because even smaller sums held presently would grow to a dollar if allowed to earn interest each year (i.e., compound interest) from the present period out to year two, three, four, or five and beyond. It should suffice to comment here that discounting back to find the present value of a future period's dollar is simply the converse process of compounding a present period's dollar up to find its value in a future period.[2]

*The Appropriate Discount Factor*

In the above example, we used 10% purely as a matter of convenience. When discounting the net cash flows of a new venture, 10% invariably will be inappropriately low. The appropriate discount rate is the rate of return that the investor could expect to achieve in a similar but alternative investment of equal risk. This is often referred to as the "opportunity" discount rate, because it refers to the investor's next-best (similar risk) opportunity to earn interest on his or her money.

The *opportunity discount rate* (ODR) thus is based on the nominal rate of interest (or more generally, the rate of return) an investor could earn elsewhere at equal risk of default by the borrower. Note that the nominal rate of interest is composed of three elements. First, there is the "real rate" of interest, which is the premium people pay to purchase things now, rather than wait until they have accumulated sufficient savings to buy the items for cash. The real rate is determined by the interaction of the overall supply and overall demand for funds in the financial markets and is typically about 3%. Second, a premium is charged by lenders to cover the expected inflation rate over the duration of the loan, because the money repaid will have lesser purchasing power per dollar when the lender regains his or her chance to spend it later. The consensus on the expected inflation rate also is reflected by the financial markets and can be deduced from the short-term government bond rates, which are considered risk free. Thus, if the 5-year government bond rate is, say, 5%, this encapsulates the real rate of about 3% and a general expectation that inflation rate will average about 2% per annum over that time horizon.

Third, a premium is charged, based on the risk that the borrower will default on the repayment of the loan. New ventures are notorious for their relatively high rate of failure, which translates into a relatively high risk of default. If 20% of businesses that are basically similar to yours have in the past failed, the investor might reasonably want to earn 20% more on every investment he or she makes in such businesses to make up for the 20% that probably will default. If the failure rate applicable to your type of business, or your business in your particular location, and incorporating all other risk factors, such as the management's lack of relevant experience, no track record yet, and so on, is even higher, say 40%, then the applicable risk premium is 40%. Add this risk premium to interest rate payable on a government bond of the same duration as the loan or the investment (say, 5%, which incorporates the real rate and the inflation rate) and the appropriate discount rate is, say, 45%.

Almost inevitably the entrepreneur and the investor will disagree on the applicable risk premium. The investor, perhaps a venture capitalist with a lot of experience funding new ventures in your industry, probably will insist on a particular discount factor. For example, "seed" projects, in which funding is needed to develop prototypes and do further market research, routinely have their projected net cash flows discounted by 50% to 70%, which involves exceptionally high risk premiums (reflecting exceptionally high risk of failure). Businesses that are further down the track, with somewhat higher probabilities of success, are routinely discounted at 30% to 50%. Even businesses with a successful track record, but who need capital to finance growth (for example, an expansion of plant and equipment, an extension of the business into new geographic markets, or related product lines, etc.), have a significant risk of default, and investors will want to discount its cash flows by 15% to 30% or even more.

It is difficult to determine the appropriate discount rate, as the information required to make such a determination is not freely available. We do know, however, that investors typically will apply as high a discount rate as you let them. Their incentive is to discount the cash flows by a higher discount rate so that the NPV is smaller. Then, the funds they are providing will constitute a larger proportion of the net present value of the business and thus translate to a larger share of the equity in the business.

If you are only dealing with one investor, that investor has the power to add a fourth element to the discount rate, namely the "monopoly" premium. So, whereas you might argue that the bond rate is only 5% and the risk of default is no more than 40%, the investor might insist on discounting your cash flows at, say, 60%, if you have no alternative potential supplier of the funding. It is always a good idea to seek several sources of funding and (in a noncombative way) attempt to play one off against the other to minimize the monopoly premium that one investor alone is able to charge.

Thus, the NPV of the cash flows generated by the business over its time horizon (say, 5 years) needs to be calculated using a discount rate that is agreeable to both the entrepreneur and the investor. Later, we shall explain how to add to these cash flows and the "end-of-horizon" valuation of the cash flows that the business is expected to generate beyond the time horizon, using the appropriate price/earnings (P/E) ratio. The NPV of all these cash flows is the present value of the business. Suppose this value is $5 million. Now, suppose that the amount to be invested by the investor in the current period is $1 million. That $1 million represents 20% of the present value of the business, and thus the supplier of those funds should be rewarded with a 20% equity stake in the business.

TABLE 8.1. NPV Calculations to Evaluate the New Venture

| Discount rate = | | | 40% | | 50% | | 71.69% | |
|---|---|---|---|---|---|---|---|---|
| | | NCF | DF | PV | DF | PV | DF | PV |
| Year | 0 | -3000 | 1.0000 | -3000.00 | 1.0000 | -3000.00 | 1.0000 | -3000.00 |
| Year | 1 | 500 | 0.7143 | 357.14 | 0.6667 | 333.33 | 0.5824 | 291.22 |
| Year | 2 | 1000 | 0.5102 | 510.20 | 0.4444 | 444.44 | 0.3392 | 339.24 |
| Year | 3 | 1500 | 0.3644 | 546.65 | 0.2963 | 444.44 | 0.1976 | 296.39 |
| Year | 4 | 2000 | 0.2603 | 520.62 | 0.1975 | 395.06 | 0.1151 | 230.17 |
| Year | 5 | 2500 | 0.1859 | 464.84 | 0.1317 | 329.22 | 0.0670 | 167.58 |
| End value | 5 | 25000 | 0.1859 | 4648.36 | 0.1317 | 3292.18 | 0.0670 | 1675.77 |
| | NPV = | | | 4047.81 | | 2238.68 | | 0.37 |

## THE INTERNAL RATE OF RETURN METHOD

Alternatively, the investor might say, for example, "I want to earn at least 60% interest compounded annually on my money." This often is referred to as a "hurdle" rate, otherwise known as the investor's *required rate of return* (RRR). Because discounting is the converse of compounding, this translates to a statement that the investor wants to discount the cash flows by 60% and still show a positive NPV.

The *internal rate of return* (IRR) is defined as the rate of discount that reduces the NPV to zero. Using a spreadsheet template we can easily keep recalculating the NPV using progressively higher discount rates until the NPV is approximately zero, and thus we would find the IRR of the business. This IRR can be interpreted as the annual compound rate of return that the initial investment in the business can generate. If the IRR is higher than the investor's RRR, then the investor should be satisfied with the investment opportunity presented, assuming he or she agrees with all the other assumptions underlying the valuation of the business.

In Table 8.1, we show the spreadsheet calculation of the NPV of a particular set of net cash flows, discounted at several discount rates, as well as the IRR calculation. Assuming the "appropriate" opportunity discount rate is 60% in this hypothetical case, we also calculate NPV with a higher and a lower ODR to show the impact of higher discount rates on NPV. In the event that the investor favors a different rate, we will have a prior idea of that impact. In the last two columns, we continue to raise the discount rate until the NPV falls to zero and thus find the IRR.

TABLE 8.2.   RRR Implied by Various Investment Multiples

| Investment Multiple | Time Horizon | | |
|---|---|---|---|
| | 3 years(%) | 5 years(%) | 10 years(%) |
| 2 | 26 | 15 | 7 |
| 3 | 44 | 25 | 12 |
| 4 | 59 | 32 | 15 |
| 5 | 71 | 38 | 17 |
| 6 | 82 | 43 | 20 |
| 7 | 91 | 48 | 21 |
| 8 | 100 | 52 | 23 |
| 9 | 108 | 55 | 25 |
| 10 | 116 | 59 | 26 |

If after calculating the IRR we find it exceeds the investor's RRR, we can then demonstrate to the investor that this investment opportunity not only meets his or her RRR but also exceeds it. This also allows us to specify the "cushion" available to the investor in terms of the extent to which his or her RRR expectations are expected to be surpassed, or alternatively, how much room there is for error in the cash flow projections before his or her RRR would not be attained.

"I WANT X TIMES MY MONEY BACK IN Y YEARS."

Alternatively, the investor might express his or her expectations in terms of a simple multiple of his or her investment over a particular time horizon. This multiple refers to "nominal" dollars, not NPV dollars. That is, the investor contributes, say, $1 million now and wants 10 times that, or $10 million dollars, back at the end of year five.

It can be shown that this is equivalent to the investor demanding a particular RRR, in this case 58.5%. That is, the initial investment of $1 million would need to compound annually at 58.5% to grow to $10 million over a period of 5 years. Thus, the investor effectively is insisting on a discount rate of 58.5% or, alternatively, stating that his or her RRR is 58.5%. Table 8.2 shows the relationship between various investment multiples and the approximate IRR necessary to achieve that multiple over horizons of 3, 5, and 10 years.

Thus, we can readily convert an investor's request for X times his or her money back in Y years to a demand for a particular RRR or hurdle rate of return. In turn, we can decompose that rate into the risk-free rate (on government bonds of the appropriate duration) and the risk premium (and perhaps also the monopoly premium). If the difference between the government bond rate and the RRR exceeds the entrepreneur's expectation of the appropriate risk premium, then negotiations can begin on that basis.

## ASSUMPTIONS UNDERLYING
## THE VALUATION

### REVENUE PROJECTIONS

The entrepreneur should base the revenue projections on explicit assumptions, which can be explained with a view to convincing the investor that these revenue projections are reasonable and attainable.

The revenue projections begin with the selling price that has been selected. This should be based on market research of what potential buyers are willing to pay, with due regard given to prices of similar products or services, if any. If the new venture offers an entirely new product or service, then the cost to the customer of satisfying the need by some other means (i.e., the price of the best substitute), or the financial burden of leaving the need unsatisfied, must be considered in the prediction of revenue. Results from trial-marketing efforts, market experiments, and/or focus-group sessions, should be produced to justify price level(s) chosen.

Then, the entrepreneur must estimate the sales volume at the chosen price level. In effect, the entrepreneur needs to postulate the location and slope of a "demand curve" for the new product and argue that the choice of the price (and associated quantity demanded) will best serve the firm's objectives. In simple economics courses we learn about the short-run profit-maximizing price, in which marginal revenue is equal to marginal cost of production. If the entrepreneur can sketch in a demand line showing how sales volume is expected to increase at lower prices (and provide evidence for these assumptions), the marginal revenue line also can be calculated.[3] Where the marginal revenue line cuts the marginal cost curve, this indicates the profit-maximizing sales volume, whereas the demand curve indicates the price that should be set to achieve this sales volume.

Alternatively, the entrepreneur's objective might be to maximize profits over a longer time horizon, say, 5 years, and this also might suit the investor, who recognizes that a relatively high short-run profit-maximizing price might induce quick entry of competitors who will compete away profits in the medium to longer term. Indeed, the entrepreneur and the investor will prefer to set a price, which maximizes the NPV of the firm over the agreed time horizon. Rather than calculate the NPV of the firm for a series of different price levels, business firms routinely use a simple mark-up pricing rule, which is expected to maximize (approximately) the NPV of the firm's cash flows.[4]


COST ASSUMPTIONS

Starting with the *cost of goods sold* (CGS), the entrepreneur must be able to demonstrate a careful and accurate projection of all costs that enter the income and cash flow statements. Manufacturing cost estimates should be obtained from two or more external (potential) suppliers and then modified to recognize the learning curve effects available to those suppliers but not yet attained by the entrepreneur. (Naturally, the entrepreneur must be careful not to give away valuable trade secrets in this process.) The shape of the learning curve is well known (it is usually an exponential function, whereby cost per unit declines by about 15% to 20% each time cumulative output is doubled), so cost projections can be made on this basis and modified as information from actual production becomes available.

Other operating expenses, including overheads and selling expenses, also must be predicted carefully and on a defensible basis, because the investor will carefully scrutinize the pro forma financial statements and may want to know the underlying rationale for any particular number. Job descriptions and workloads for each employee must be considered, to demonstrate that employee numbers have not been underestimated. This analysis also will allow the entrepreneur to argue that some tasks should be outsourced, at least initially, to conserve cash balances.

## ACCOUNTING CONVENTIONS

There are a variety of accounting conventions, which are legal and permissible, regarding depreciation of purchased assets. Whereas depreciation has no impact on cash balances, it does influence the income statement, and different treatments can cause the profit (or loss) to be understated or overstated. The *straight line* depreciation method apportions the capital cost of the asset (less its estimated salvage value) equally over the projected life of the asset. *Declining balance* methods charge a constant proportion of the (declining) balance against revenues each period and thus have greater impact on profits in early years than in later years. Essentially, the entrepreneur and the investor should agree on the depreciation convention used if they are to agree on the valuation of the firm, because the "end-of-horizon" valuation of the firm's future profit potential depends on the year five profit level.

Next, the entrepreneur might wish to capitalize, rather than expense, some initial expenditures, such as research and development cost, registration and licensing fees, and so on. If these are capitalized, they will be depreciated over some time horizon using either a straight line or declining balance method. Again, the entrepreneur and the investor must agree on the treatment of these items if they are to agree on the valuation of the business.

The third item we shall mention is the valuation of inventories. When the prices of components vary over time, they might be valued on either a FIFO (*first-in-first-out*) or LIFO (*last-in-first-out*) basis. When component costs are increasing over time, LIFO more accurately values items that although purchased previously at a lower invoice cost nonetheless would cost more to replace in inventory at the current time. With the increasing prevalence of JIT (*just-in-time*) inventory management, this is less of a problem, of course, but again, the entrepreneur and the investor must agree on the basis for inventory valuation if they subsequently are to agree on the valuation of the business.

## TIME HORIZON SELECTED

The typical time horizon used is 5 years, although a case can be argued for either a longer or shorter planning period in specific cases. For example, a "fad" item might complete its entire product life cycle within 3 years, whereas a new biotech venture seeking "seed" funding might not even begin earning sales revenues until year three and face a product life cycle that militates for a 10-year time horizon.

If the sales' growth (or product life cycle) still is rising steeply at the end of the 5th year, it is in the entrepreneur's interest to argue for a longer time horizon. Using a longer time horizon will admit into the NPV calculation even larger net cash flows in the sixth, seventh, and subsequent years. Even though the discount factors applied to these cash flows will be smaller, their inclusion will increase the NPV (and the IRR) if the sales growth curve is rising steeply. More important, the "end-of-horizon" valuation of the business (which is the product of the last year's profit and the price/earnings, P/E, ratio), will be higher.

The investor may disagree with the time horizon selected, of course, perhaps preferring to harvest his or her interest in the business after only 3 or 4 years and thus want to value the business over a shorter time horizon. The entrepreneur needs to be aware of this potential area for disagreement over the valuation of the business and hence for the share of equity going to the investor.

## THE PRICE/EARNINGS RATIO SELECTED

As indicated earlier, the "end-of-horizon" valuation of the firm's future profit typically is done by multiplying the last year of the time horizon's profit by the applicable P/E ratio. But what is the appropriate P/E ratio? New firms with fantastic growth prospects that list on the stock exchange may trade at stock prices that, in aggregate, value the company at, say, 30 or even 50 times the current profit levels. Conversely, businesses without very exciting growth prospects, such as a dental practice, might be sold at a value only two or three times annual profits.

The P/E ratio applied makes a large difference to the value of the firm and thus to the share of owners' equity, which should be allocated to the investor in exchange for his or her cash contribution. In Table 8.3, we show the share of equity required for the specific example of an investor

TABLE 8.3.  Share of Equity Required to Achieve Several RRRs Under Different
            P/E Ratios

| *Price/Earnings Ratio* | *Required Rate of Return (percentage)* | | |
|---|---|---|---|
| | 40 | 50 | 60 |
| 6 | 8.96 | 12.66 | 17.49 |
| 8 | 6.72 | 9.49 | 13.11 |
| 10 | 5.38 | 7.59 | 10.49 |
| 12 | 4.48 | 6.33 | 8.74 |
| 14 | 3.84 | 5.42 | 7.49 |
| 16 | 3.36 | 4.75 | 6.55 |
| 18 | 2.99 | 4.22 | 5.24 |
| 20 | 2.69 | 3.80 | 4.77 |

N.B. This is for a specific example in which the investor contributes $1 million dollars, receives no dividends, and exits at the end of Year 5 by selling his or her share of the stock, and in which Year 5 profits are assumed to be $10 million.

who invests $1 million, wants to exit at the end of Year 5 achieving a particular RRR, and expects year five profits to be $10 million, for a variety of P/E ratios shown.

From Table 8.3, it is evident that the P/E ratio selected has tremendous impact on the share of equity that an investor will require to attain his or her RRR (or investment multiple). The entrepreneur has a strong incentive to argue for a relatively high P/E, whereas the investor's incentive is quite the opposite. Clearly, they must agree on the P/E to be applied if they are to agree (amicably) on the share of equity going to the investor.

The entrepreneur should assemble evidence from the financial markets to support his or her claim for a particular P/E. If similar companies are listed on the stock exchange and have recently reported profits, their P/Es can be calculated readily. Or, if you can argue that your company is in the same stage that a similar company was in several years before, you might use that company's P/E (several years ago) as the best approximation. Finally, if other firms recently have acquired similar companies, the acquisition price will be some multiple of their recent profits, thus suggesting a market evaluation of the P/E ratio.[5]

Without such hard evidence of market-determined P/E ratios, the entrepreneur will be at the mercy of the investor. Even with such evidence, there is likely to be a debate about whether or not your business is strictly comparable to the others you have identified. It is perhaps more fruitful to find evidence of companies that are more or less similar in most important respects and then suggest a P/E several points lower than the examples found elsewhere. In our experience, investors will accept claims that the appropriate P/E ratio is 10 (or even 12) for new ventures prior to launch but will balk at 15 and 20, even if you can point to very similar companies trading in that range.

In all such cases, it is surely better to have the investor think your financials are perhaps a little too conservative, rather than thinking they are overly optimistic. Being more conservative (in terms of the financial projections) exhibits a sense of prudence that will be comforting to the investor whose funds are put at risk.

## RECONCILING THE ASSUMPTIONS AND NEGOTIATING THE DEAL

### THE NEGOTIATION PROCESS

In the business plan, the subsequent presentation to the investor, or both the entrepreneur normally will "ask" for a specific level of funding and "offer" a specific share in the company. This offer should be regarded as an opening claim, because the investor certainly will treat it as such. Thus, the entrepreneur should consider making an offer that is based on a set of assumptions that he or she expects will be not quite acceptable to the investor. For example, recognizing that the appropriate discount rate probably should be 50% and the P/E should be 10, the entrepreneur might make the offer based on a discount rate of 45% and a P/E of 12. This may allow the entrepreneur to gracefully give ground and be "argued up" to an equity offer that he or she feels is appropriate.

But it is perhaps much more likely that the investor will make a counteroffer to provide the funding for what may seem like an outrageous share of the business. Again, this is almost certainly an ambit claim, even if couched in "take it or leave it" terms. At this point, the two ends of the spectrum are defined and the negotiation process begins, with the objective being to reach an intermediate solution that is agreeable to both parties.

### Establishing Points of
### Agreement and Disagreement

A good starting point is to proceed through the various issues outlined in this chapter and establish points of agreement. Do you agree on the discount rate? Do you agree on the P/E ratio? Do you agree on the time horizon? Do you agree on the revenue projections? Do you agree on the cost assumptions? If the entrepreneur and the investor can agree on at least some of these points, then it narrows the field of disagreement to the remaining points.

### Dealing With Disagreement

If there is disagreement on the revenue projections, for example, do you agree on the price level proposed? on the sales volume assumed? Do you agree on the rate of increase of sales in subsequent years? Do you agree with our assumptions about the reactions of existing rivals? Do you agree with our assumption about the timing of entry of new competitors? On the cost side, are there points of disagreement? Which lines on the cash budget, income statement, or both are not considered realistic or accurate by the investor?

When the entire set of assumptions is agreed on between the two parties, there will be a set of financial statements agreeable to both parties. If not, go back to see which assumption(s) is(are) causing the disagreement and renegotiate these points, giving ground if you need to (and have no alternative supplier of funds waiting in the wings). Once the NPV of the business is agreed on, it is a simple matter to find what proportion of that NPV is the current period cash contribution to be made by the investor. If it is 28.25%, then that is the share of equity that should be given to the investor for that funding.

### Does the Investor Supply
### More Than Money?

If two or more investors each were willing to supply the funds on your terms, wouldn't you want to choose among them on the basis of what else they bring to the table? Of course, because investors have the potential to bring more than just money to the business. Ideally, you want an investor with relevant industry and market experience, useful contacts, and perhaps celebrity status or other brand name recognition. It also might be preferable to find an investor who wants to be more passive, rather than actively monitoring your day-to-day activities (or vice versa). In effect, you are forming a partnership with the investor that, it is hoped, will endure for many years and subsequent rounds of financing. You want that investor's expertise and experience to be there when you seek it, to give you guidance and support as needed.

If the investor brings more to the table than mere money, you should be willing to give more equity than is suggested by the simple "proportion of NPV" rule, because the nonmonetary items listed previously did not enter (or were probably incompletely captured in) the NPV calculations. In effect, you would be giving "sweat equity" to the investor for his or her future efforts to assist your business, in addition to the equity justifiable simply on financial grounds.

## CREATIVE FINANCING

### FUNDING IN STAGES AS NEEDED

If all the money is not required initially, it is usually desirable to divide the funding into two or more distinct stages. Doing so usually will reduce the cost of funding. For simple debt funding, later loans should be obtainable at a lower interest rate due to a reduced risk premium, because the business will have demonstrated that it has survived and that at least some of its projections were accurate. For equity funding, the investor's RRR should be reduced significantly for the same reason. Thus, you may be able to agree on a somewhat reduced discount factor to be applied to the annual profits. Further, if annual sales and profits are projected to increase, and the time horizon stays at, say, 5 years, the (higher) NCF and profits of year six enter the calculation for the first time—raising the NPV substantially, it is hoped. Thus, the funds required will be a smaller percentage of the NPV.

## DEBT VERSUS EQUITY

Entrepreneurs sometimes cling to their equity against their own best interests, perhaps based on their reluctance to be accountable to someone else. Although it is a natural extension of their typically strong desire for independence and control, entrepreneurs must always remember the old adage that "X% of something is better than 100% of nothing." As an alternative to "giving away" equity, and having exhausted all sources of personal and family funding, such entrepreneurs often turn to debt funding from banks or other lenders. But debt usually requires periodic repayment of at least the interest on the loan, which puts even greater stress on cash flow in the early stages of the venture.

From finance theory, we know that there is an optimal mix of debt and equity in the mature firm, but for the new venture, debt should not be considered unless sales already have begun and are trending upward and the entrepreneur feels confident there will be sufficient cash flows to comfortably service the debt. Bridging loans for working capital to buy raw materials and produce output that has been ordered are a good case for debt funding, of course. There is a middle ground, namely, convertible debt, which is funding that begins like debt but allows the lender the option to convert to an equity position in the new venture.[6]

## VOTING VERSUS NONVOTING STOCK

If the entrepreneur strongly prefers to maintain managerial control, and at the same time the investor is content to have a passive role in the business, the equity issued to the investor might be "nonvoting" stock. This is another "negotiating chip" that the entrepreneur or the investor might introduce into the negotiation process in an attempt to reach an amicable agreement.

## MANAGEMENT CONTRACTS
## AND PERFORMANCE CRITERIA

Even when the investor has a majority share of the (voting) equity, and thus could remove the entrepreneur from any and all management roles if this was deemed necessary, it may be in the investor's best interest to provide the entrepreneur with a management contract that prevents this outcome, as long as certain predetermined performance criteria are achieved. The threat of losing management control should spur the entrepreneur to manage to the utmost of his or her ability, to the benefit of all shareholders. Conversely, the entrepreneur might only be prepared to give up more than 50% of the firm if he or she can maintain management control of the business.

TAKING OPTIONS ON
MANAGEMENT'S SHARE OF EQUITY

If the investor wants control in the event that things do not proceed according to plan, the entrepreneur might gamble part of his or her share of equity on his or her ability to achieve the financial results projected in the plan or some other minimally acceptable level of financial results. That is, the entrepreneur and the investor might reach an agreement that if, and only if, the managers cannot achieve specified performance targets in the first N years, then X% of the manager's equity reverts to the investor. The investor then would attain control and potentially replace some or all of the management team.

What level of financial performance should be specified in a deal like this? One interesting approach is to say that the management should be able to attain at least the "worst-case" scenario results or face charges of incompetence. The "worst scenario" should be viewed as a scenario that is based on a series of specified assumptions about external conditions and forces (for example, sales 30% below expectations due to a macro-economic downturn, price 10% lower due to entry of competition, cost 15% higher due to increases in materials costs, and so on.) Competent management still is assumed in the worst scenario.

If management does not make the worst-scenario financial figures, this will be due to either unforeseen adversity, management incompetence, or some combination. And it might be argued that more competent managers might have foreseen the unforeseen adversity! Thus, setting the worst-case financials as the trigger point for the reversion of equity (and control) to the investor will spur the management to keep their eyes open and to respond vigorously to adversity. If they fail to achieve these targets, they always might argue that no manager could have foreseen what happened, and the investor might agree and allow them to retain control. Alternatively, and preferably, the parties might agree at the outset that an independent third party (such as an accounting firm) might act as the arbiter who decides whether or not management acted competently under the circumstances and, thus, whether or not the equity and control should revert to the investor.

We are not advocating that these complex terms be immediately offered to the investor. Rather, they may be offered as "deadlock breakers" if negotiations reach the point at which the investor wants control in the event that his or her investment seems to be endangered but the entrepreneur wants to retain control and firmly believes that the financial results are attainable. This particular creative solution might be the key that unlocks the deadlock.

## SLIDING SCALE AGREEMENTS
## FOR MANAGEMENT'S SHARE

Similarly, to break a deadlock, management might agree to "earn" their designated share of equity in specified increments, if they can deliver a series of financial results specified in a formal agreement. Thus, attainment of year one targets might give them 50% of their anticipated share, attainment of year two targets might add another 25%, and attainment of year three targets might bring them to 100% of their designated share.

Alternatively, management might receive, say, 30% of the equity if the business makes $1 million profit (in the first year or over N years), 40% if it makes $2 million profit, 51% if it makes over $3 million profit, for example. Management might agree to this because they firmly believe the latter result can be achieved, whereas investors might agree to this because their rate of return expectations (from dividends, growth in the value of their equity, or both) would be met in all three scenarios.

## CONCLUSION

In this chapter, we discussed the valuation of the new venture and how to calculate the share of equity that should fairly go to the investor. We pointed out the main places in which disagreement between the entrepreneur and the investor can arise and suggested ways to reach agreement. In effect, the entrepreneur either must convince the investor of the validity of the assumptions underlying the business valuation, seek an alternative source of equity capital and start the information and persuasion process all over again, or reach a graceful compromise that assures that the funds are actually forthcoming.

## NOTES

1. Timmons, J. A. (1994). *New venture creation: Entrepreneurship for the 21st century* (4th ed.). Boston, MA: Irwin.

2. The future value at a point one year hence (FV1) of a present value (PV) is $FV1 = PV(1+r)$ where r represents the rate of interest. Thus, the FV1 of $1 is equal to $1(1.1) = $1.10 in one year (when $r = 10\%$). If that future value were to be reinvested for another year, it would earn 10% on the principal and the interest already earned. That is, $FV2 = PV(1+r)(1+r) = PV(1+r)^2$. If we were to reinvest the money for a third year we would find $FV3 = PV(1+r)(1+r)(1+r) = PV(1+r)^3$. More generally, the future value of a dollar to be invested for n years (where n might be 1,2,3,4,5, etc.) at r percent interest is $FVn = PV(1+r)^n$. Conversely, the present value of a dollar to be received n years into the future is $PV = FVn/(1+r)n$. Note that the value of $1/(1+r)n$ is known as the "discount factor." When $n = 1$ (and $r = 10\%$), it is equal to $1/(1.1)1 = 0.9091$, consistent with the "91 cent" example used in the text. Note further that it is $1/(1.1)^2 = 0.8264$ when $n = 2$, and $1/(1.1)^3 = 0.7513$ when $n = 3$, and so on. Thus, amounts to be received further into the future are multiplied by progressively smaller discount factors.

3. See any basic economics text.

4. We have only touched on the analysis that can be carried out on the demand side and a new venture's pricing policies. For more information, we refer you to Besanko, D., Dranove, D., & Shanley, M. (1996). *Economics of strategy.* New York: John Wiley.

5. A market evaluation of the P/E ratio is not always available (for example, pioneers). Under such circumstances, the assumed ratio is likely to be questioned during negotiation.

6. The deal might include the capitalization of the interest, such that the borrower makes no periodic payments on the loan until the point of its repayment or conversion to equity. Convertible debt may be attractive to the investor who wants periodic interest payments or who wants to have high priority among creditors in the event that the business become illiquid but at the same time would like to share in the "blue sky" of the business. Convertible debt allows the investor access to the "upside potential" at the same time offering protection from the downside risk.

# 9 | Summary and Conclusions

This book is designed to help entrepreneurs better prepare and present themselves to investors for the purpose of raising equity capital. It is not a substitute for a book on "how to write a business plan." Rather, it is complementary to books of that genre.

This book takes the wider view that investors invest in businesses and people, rather than in new products or services. Thus, it takes the perspective that the investor is looking for more than just a good business plan. The investor is looking for a business that is "investor ready" and that corresponds with the investor's own preferences for location and industry as well as one that seems to promise a lucrative investment possibility.

"Investor readiness" means the business concept has been properly thought through and subjected to scrutiny by management trying to view the business and the management team through the eyes of the investor.

We also take the view that the business plan cannot stand on its own and that many a good business plan (perhaps written by someone else) has failed to gain funding because the management team were unable to successfully complete the second and third stages of the communication process, namely, the presentation and the question-and-answer session. Thus, we devoted a chapter to the art of writing a compelling business plan and another to the art of making a presentation to the investor and subsequently surviving the question-and-answer session.

Once the presentation to the investor has been made, it is not simply a case of wait for the investor to accept your offer of equity in the business. Instead, the offer needs to be properly based on a defensible valuation of the business, and the entrepreneur needs to be armed with details of the valuation and prepared to negotiate with the investor if a deal is to be struck.

We will now summarize the findings of this book, chapter by chapter. For those who have turned directly to the end of the book to find out what it is about, be warned that there is no substitute for the journey through the book. You will find out where the destination is, but you may not know how to get there on your own. You are strongly advised to go back and learn your way through the chapters.

## SOURCES OF EARLY-STAGE
## VENTURE CAPITAL

In Chapter 1, we found that debt is hard to arrange for a new business with neither tangible assets nor reliable cash flow to assuage the doubts of the typical banker, so selling equity shares in the business is the most promising source of new venture funding. After self-funding (or boot-strapping), the entrepreneur or management team typically will seek the help of family and friends, who tend to invest or lend on the basis of trust rather than any cold hard scrutiny of the business itself.

Business angels form the next stratum of potential funding for the new venture and tend to fill in the gap between self or friends or family funding and funding by venture capitalists. Often, wealthy professionals with excess cash to invest, business angels tend to "take the new venture under their wing" and offer more than money, including business advice and access to a network of other angels and business advisors.

As distinct from the informal equity capital market populated by business angels, venture capital firms constitute the formal equity capital market for new ventures. They tend to not invest in smaller deals or "seed" and "start-up" stage funding, preferring to invest in businesses that already are showing good results and need funding to grow and proceed toward an initial public offering of equity.

The main lesson in this chapter is perhaps that an entrepreneur might waste a lot of money, time, and emotion trying to "sell" his or her business plan to investors who are unlikely to invest, not because it is not a lucrative investment opportunity but because they have established

TABLE 9.1. Checklist—Sources of Early-Stage Financing

1. Is debt funding possible? Do you have assets for collateral, and/or cashflow to support repayments?

2. Is personal, family, or friends funding possible? Can you possibly "bootstrap" the business until a later point of time?

3. Is the amount required large enough to interest venture capital firms, or should you seek a business angel?

4. Have you identified venture capital firms (or angels) who invest in this type of business, in your geographic area?

5. Can you arrange a referral to the investor by somebody the investor trusts and respects?

6. Are you and the investor compatible in terms of personality fit? Can you foresee a long-term relationship with this investor?

7. What else does the investor bring to the table besides money? How extensive and useful are the investor's network?

8. Is the investor a useful source of management, technical advice, or both?

9. Does the investor want to be actively involved in the business, or is he or she content to be a passive investor?

10. Have you other potential investors "on the line" to avoid exploitation by a monopoly supplier?

preferences as to the type and location of businesses in which they invest. Therefore, the management team needs to seek out investors (whether angels or venture capital firms) that are interested in the particular area in which the business plans to operate. They may do this directly, or indirectly, via a series of contacts, but they must do it to save themselves unnecessary expenditure of funds, time, and emotion on pitching their plan to investors who are not really sufficiently interested (or who would be too difficult to convince). Sources of early-stage financing are shown in Table 9.1.

## ROLES AND EQUITY SHARES
## IN THE NEW VENTURE

We then proceeded, in Chapter 2, to an examination of the structure of the business ownership prior to the new investor coming on board. We urged the business to "get its house in order" before inviting the investor to come and see inside. Inasmuch as there is such great potential for role conflict in the new venture, the equity shares of the people serving in the typical roles of inventor, manager, and investor must be carefully considered and established to minimize conflict and encourage optimal performance from all parties to the new business.

We advocate that an "ownership plan" be made explicit from the very outset so that misunderstandings between and amongst role players are minimized. All new entrants to the business would join, knowing who owns what share of the equity and what the other parties expectations are of them. Potential dilution of share holdings as more capital is required would be foreseen under a protocol established for making financial calls on equity holders. Agreed shares might be allocated over time as performance targets are met, rather than in toto initially, to avoid subsequent conflict over who is not pulling their weight.

We also advise the entrepreneur or management team to seek funding earlier rather than later and from multiple sources of funding, to avoid being exploited by a monopoly supplier of funds at the 11th hour as desperation takes over. The business also should be seeking more than money, inasmuch as the best kind of money comes complete with managerial expertise, industry contacts, celebrity endorsements, and/or a willingness to be a passive investor. It was also advised that the management team should clearly specify their expectations with regard to those of the investors involved in the business, if any. Roles and equity shares in a new business are illustrated in Table 9.2.


## EVALUATE THE BUSINESS CONCEPT
## FROM THE INVESTOR'S PERSPECTIVE


To be more attractive to the investor, the business needs to be exactly the kind of thing the investor is looking for. In Chapter 3, we considered the types of businesses generally sought by investors, and we discussed the importance of superior value, the service of long-felt needs, the importance of follow-up products, and of a proprietary position using intellectual property protection.

We then considered the liability of newness and its determinants, which were novelty (or ignorance) in consumption, production, and/or management. This led to a discussion of risk recognition and risk reduction strategies that must be considered before the typical investor will be sufficiently comfortable to invest in the entrepreneur's business. The

TABLE 9.2. Checklist—Roles and Equity Shares in the New Venture

1. What are the strategic assets of the business? Are these a sustainable competitive advantage of the business?
2. Who owns or holds the strategic assets of the business, and what share of ownership has been allocated to these parties?
3. Who deserves some equity allocation on the basis of "sweat equity," and what shares should be allocated to them?
4. If there is still "sweat equity" work to be done, is there a plan for sequential allocation of that equity?
5. Who is going to write the formal business plan, and how is that person or group to be remunerated for this task?
6. Are the managers to be taken on as equity partners (to better align their incentives) or as simple employees?
7. Are the managers to have a "call option" on their equity in case they fail to deliver the expected results?
8. Is equity to be allocated to any other stakeholder or external party, in return for any other consideration?
9. Is there an explicit protocol in place for financial calls and an explicit criterion for external investors?
10. Is there an explicit statement of the expectation concerning the investor's involvement in day-to-day operations?

evaluation procedures of the business from the viewpoint of the investor are in Table 9.3.

## EVALUATE THE MANAGEMENT TEAM
## FROM THE INVESTOR'S PERSPECTIVE

Inasmuch as investors invest in people rather than products, a promising new product or service concept is not enough to obtain funding. In Chapter 4, we noted that the new venture also must have a management team that stands up to scrutiny from an investor's perspective. The investor will want to see a diverse but complementary team of highly qualified individuals with sufficient relevant experience. Preferably, these managers also should have invested a significant proportion of their own wealth in the venture, to ensure that their incentive structure is sufficiently aligned with that of the investor.

Boards of directors and advisory groups also were discussed as a means of bringing expertise into the business to bolster the talents of the

TABLE 9.3. Checklist—Evaluate the Business From the Investor's Viewpoint

---

1. Is your new venture within the investor's area of technical and geographic interest?

2. Does your new product or service provide superior value—better quality, lower price, or both?

3. Is there a "long-felt" need for your product or service that is well appreciated by the market at large?

4. Do you hold a proprietary position in the market that will give your business a sustainable competitive advantage?

5. Do you have follow-up products ready to roll out, or at least in the process of prototype development?

6. Do you already have a "track record" of sales with your new product or service?

7. To what degree is the new product or service novel to consumers?

8. To what degree is the new product or service novel in production?

9. To what degree do the managers have prior experience in the marketing and management of a product or service like this?

10. What risk reduction strategies have been put in place to offset perceived risks facing the business?

---

management team without burdening the business with additional full-time salaries. Finally, novelty to the management team also was discussed in some detail, and it became clear why investors prefer to see considerable experience in the relevant market, inasmuch as this significantly (and positively) affects the probability of survival for the business. The investor's evaluation of the management team is shown in Table 9.4.

## THE THREE-STAGE
## COMMUNICATION STRATEGY

It was stressed that the business plan is merely the first stage in a three-stage communication process. After the investor has read the business plan, he or she will invite the entrepreneurial team to make a presentation and participate in a question-and-answer session. The presentation and Q&A session provide an opportunity for the investor to clarify any remaining doubts and gain further information about the quality of the management team and the business opportunity.

In Chapter 5, we concluded that the main role of the business plan is to impress the investor, such that the entrepreneur is invited to make a presentation. The main purpose of the presentation is to reinforce in the

TABLE 9.4. Checklist—Evaluate the Management Team From the Investor's
Perspective

| | |
|---|---|
| 1. | Does the CEO have a track record of visionary leadership or exhibit the qualities of leadership plus management skills? |
| 2. | Does the management team include someone with strong qualifications and substantial experience in marketing? |
| 3. | Does the management team include someone with strong qualifications in accounting and financial management? |
| 4. | Does the business have the necessary technical expertise in the area(s) critical to the success of the business? |
| 5. | Is the management team complementary in their expertise and skills, and have they worked together as a team before? |
| 6. | Does the management team have a significant equity share and reasonable salaries to align their motives with investors? |
| 7. | Have the members of the management team invested significant "hurt money" in the business? |
| 8. | Is there a competent board of advisors in place to assist the management team? |
| 9. | Is the business novel to management in any way—does the management team have relevant experience in similar industries and markets? |
| 10. | Does management recognize the risks involved, and have they undertaken any strategies to reduce these risks? |

investor's mind the viability of the business and the competency of the management team. The main purpose of the final stage, the Q&A session, is to satisfy any remaining doubts the investor might have and to further impress the investor with the business acumen and thorough preparation of the management team. Steps in developing a three-stage strategy are found in Table 9.5.

## WRITE A COMPELLING BUSINESS PLAN

In Chapter 6, we concentrated on the presentation of the business plan. The structure and sequencing of the material in the plan certainly have an impact on the investor's perception of how good the plan (and consequently the business) really is. After regaling the virtues of parsimony and persistence, and the necessity to have the plan read by external parties and to be rewritten again and again in an iterative process, we

TABLE 9.5.   Checklist—Devising Your Three-Stage Communication Strategy

1. Do you know what the target investor usually looks for in an investment opportunity?
2. List five reasons why the investor would be interested in investing in your business.
3. List five benefits that the investor would bring to your business.
4. What is the main purpose of your business plan (as part of the communication process with the investor)?
5. What is the main purpose of your presentation (as part of the communication process with the investor)?
6. What aspects of your business will not be covered in detail in your business plan but saved for another stage?
7. Which of those aspects will be saved for the question-and-answer session for detailed discussion and why?
8. List 20 examples within your business plan and presentation in which you have been admirably parsimonious.
9. Argue that you have achieved a logical flow of ideas throughout your business plan.
10. Argue that you have built and maintained investor interest in you business plan and in your presentation.

recommended the use of visual aids in the business plan for better "readability."

A suggested sequence of topics, and a suggested allocation of the 25-page "budget" limit over these topics, was made. Considerable time was spent on the executive summary, because it is critical to inducing the

TABLE 9.6.   Checklist—Write a Compelling Business Plan

1. Is your business plan 25 pages or less, with 15 or fewer pages of appendixes?
2. Has it been revised several times and subjected to critical review by external readers?
3. Is your business plan appropriately punctuated by tables, graphs, and charts, rather than just pages of turgid prose?
4. Have you followed a "page budget" for your business plan to appropriately weight the elements of your business plan?
5. Does your executive summary say all the required things and inspire interest and enthusiasm in the reader?
6. What is the stated mission and objectives of your business, and what (broad definition) business are you in?
7. What are the main components of your marketing strategy and your marketing mix?
8. Have you carefully considered all aspects of production and logistics?
9. Have you conducted scenario and sensitivity analyses on your financial projections?
10. Have you explicitly recognized the risks facing your business and put in place a series of risk reduction strategies?

investor to read on through the plan. Then, suggestions were made for the presentation and content of the remainder of the business plan and the appendixes. The components of a compelling business plan are in Table 9.6.

## SUCCESSFULLY PRESENTING AND DEFENDING YOUR BUSINESS PLAN

In Chapter 7, after some words of advice on dress, demeanor, and who should participate in the presentation to the investor, a plan was put forward that divided the time available into a series of tasks that should be accomplished. The presentation was effectively divided into three main sections: about one third on the new product or business concept, about one third on the competence of the management team, and the remaining one third on the financials.

The three main tasks in the presentation are to get the investors excited about the new product or service concept, convince them that the management team adds substantial value to the business, and communicate the financial viability of the new venture. Having achieved this, it simply remains to pitch "the deal" and begin the negotiation process, which effectively begins with the Q&A session. After giving some advice on how questions should be answered, a series of potential questions were offered for the management team to ponder and formulate their "best answers." Steps for a successful presentation and defense of the business plan are outlined in Table 9.7.

## VALUING THE BUSINESS AND NEGOTIATING THE DEAL

To agree on the appropriate share of equity for the investor, the parties must effectively agree on the value of the business in net present value terms. In Chapter 8, we noted that the invested capital will simply represent a proportion of the business's NPV, and this proportion represents the amount of equity transferred to the investor. The value of the business depends on six major assumptions. Disagreement on these

TABLE 9.7.   Checklist—Successfully Presenting and Defending
            Your Business Plan

---

1.  What are the three main purposes of your presentation?

2.  Who will participate in your presentation and why?

3.  What strategies will you employ to look like a team and for the CEO to look like a good leader of the team?

4.  How much time have you allocated to each of the three main objectives of the presentation?

5.  What use have you made of multimedia in your presentation, and are you sure this is not overdone?

6.  What strategies have you used to get the investor excited about your new product or service concept?

7.  What have you done to convince the investor that your management team adds value to the business proposition?

8.  List five marketing questions that you anticipate receiving a question on in the Q&A session.

9.  List five technical questions that you anticipate receiving a question on in the Q&A session.

10. List five financial and risk questions that you anticipate receiving a question on in the Q&A session.

---

underlying assumptions means that the parties will disagree over the valuation of the business and over the appropriate equity share.

Understanding the basis for the valuation allows the entrepreneur or management team to reconcile the investor's counteroffer in terms of different perspectives on the underlying issues. Negotiation can proceed on that basis, and agreement may be achieved more readily than if neither side is fully aware of the underlying rationale for the business valuation. Finally, some negotiating "chips" were suggested that might serve to bring the parties into agreement, even though their view of the future is markedly different. Considerations when valuing the business and negotiating the deal are shown in Table 9.8.

## CONCLUSION

This book is designed to help entrepreneurs bring their businesses to an advanced state of "investor readiness," such that the probability of attracting early-stage funding is significantly increased. We trust that it

TABLE 9.8.  Checklist—Valuing the Business and Negotiating the Deal

1. What discount rate have you used, and what is your justification for using that rate?

2. Would the NPV of your business change markedly if the time horizon was shortened or lengthened by 2 years?

3. What P/E ratio have you utilized, and how have you justified your selection of that ratio?

4. How sensitive are your NPV and IRR figures to the price level and associated sales volumes assumed?

5. How sensitive is your NPV to the cost levels assumed—what would happen if costs were 20% higher?

6. If the investor says, "I want at least eight times my money back in 5 years" what IRR is necessary to generate this?

7. What ground are you prepared to yield from your (ambit claim) equity offer and the "bottom line" offer to the investor?

8. How do you plan to achieve agreement with the investor if your valuations of the business differ markedly?

9. Is it feasible to seek your funding in stages to reduce the amount of equity you must give up in total? Why or why not?

10. What contract are you willing to enter concerning your management performance to keep the investor's share of equity down?

will help you, if you read it carefully and try to incorporate into your business (and your business plan and presentation) the elements covered in the book and particularly those issues summarized in the eight tables in this chapter.

If this book does help firms set up more viable businesses and obtain funding with less time spent and less angst experienced, it will have served its purpose. And by so doing, it will serve to raise employment, business productivity, and the standard of living in nations around the world, by which standards it might be called a success.

# Index

Accountants, 60
Accounting conventions, 145
Advertising, 48-49, 52. *See also*
    Promotion strategy
Advisory groups, 64, 68, 159-160
Agents. *See* Principal-agent problem
Allocation of equity. *See* Equity allocation
Angels. *See* Business angels
Appendices, 84, 112
Approval, regulatory, 104-105
Arbitrators, 32
Arimasu Food Corp., 101
Articles of association, 30
Asian Foods Inc., 72, 100-102
Ask and offer:
    in the business plan, 85(table), 112
    in the presentation, 121(table),
        126-127
    in the Q&A session, 134
    negotiation process and, 148-153
Assumptions:
    for valuing the business, 136-137,
        143-148, 163-164
    in the business plan, 85(table), 96, 110,
        111
Attorneys, 36-37, 60
Availability, and novelty, 48

Baan Co., 11
Balance sheets, 111
Baskin and Robbins, 44

Ben and Jerry's, 44
Boards of directors, 159-160
    investors on, 6, 11
    quality management and, 63, 68
Bond rate, 143
Bootstrapping, 4, 46, 156
Boston Economics, 5
Brand equity, 104
Brand names, 45, 52, 114
Break-even analysis, 112
Breeze Technology Inc., 43
    business plan examples from, 86-87,
        97-98
Briazz, 1, 2
Business angels, 3(table), 9-11, 156
    hours invested by, 11
    how to contact, 12-13
    matchmaking services for, 13-14
    preferences of, 12
    profile of typical, 10(table)
    statistics on, 10, 11, 12, 13, 14
    *See also* Investors
Business plan:
    as a living document, 82
    as an iterative process, 81-82, 161
    brevity in, 76, 81, 83
    checklist for, 162(table)
    color in, 84
    competitions for, 13
    components of, 84-112
    cost of, 22
    critical review of, 82

document design for, 83-84
examples of, 85-94, 97-103, 105,
    108-111
fonts for, 83
importance of, 80, 113
length of, 76, 84-85(table), 162
logical flow in, 77, 81
modified for target audiences, 78
page budget for, 84-85(table), 162
proprietary information in, 114
purpose of, 74, 78, 160
strategic omissions/inclusions in, 75-
    76
ultimate goal of, 74
visual aids in, 77-78, 83, 162
white space in, 83-84
writing of, 161-163
Business planner, 22, 23-24

Call options, 27, 30
Calls, financial, 30, 32-33, 37
Canada, business angels in, 10
Capital, early-stage. *See* Financing,
    early-stage
Capital gain, 110
Capitalization versus expensing, 145
Carnelian, Inc., 23
Cash conservation, 66, 67
Cash flow:
    debt versus equity and, 2
    equity allocation and, 22
    in the business plan, 100, 102, 111
    marketing mix and, 100, 102
    NPV analysis and, 138-140, 141
Cash flow statement, 111
CGS. *See* Cost of goods sold
Chief executive officer (CEO):
    business angel as, 11
    during presentation, 119
    during Q&A session, 129-132
    leadership of, 59, 68, 129, 130
    quality of, 59, 68
    replacement of, 6
Chief financial officer, 60, 68
    during presentation, 119
    during Q&A session, 129
Chief marketing officer, 59-60, 68
    during presentation, 119

during Q&A session, 129
Co-investments, 6, 7
Coca-Cola, 45
Colorado Capital Alliance, 13-14
Comfort, of investors, 41
Communication strategy, 70, 73-79, 114,
    160-161
    checklist for, 162(table)
Company overview, 84(table), 89-90
Competitive advantage, 93, 98, 105
    novelty and, 49, 51
    proprietary position and, 44
    questions on, 134
    value and, 42-43
Competitive positioning, 98-103
Competitor analysis, 85(table), 94-98
Confirmed orders, 47
Conflict:
    in equity allocation, 20-27, 32
    in roles, 157-158
    negotiation and, 149
    reduction of, 27-36
Consultants:
    cost of, 22
    for arbitration, 32
    for business planning, 22, 23
    for financial management, 66
Consumers, 99. *See also* Customers
Contracting:
    of financial services, 60
    of manufacturing, 53, 67
    of marketing, 52
    of specialist services, 60
Control issues, 71. *See also* Involvement
Convertible debt, 137
Corporation structure, 36
Cost curve, 144
Cost of goods sold (CGS), 144
Costs:
    assumptions on, 144-145
    novelty and, 48, 49, 50-51
    of advertising, 49
    of business plan, 22
    of consultants, 22
    of financing, 150
    of manufacturing, 106, 144
    of searching, 48-49
    of switching, 48, 49, 52
Criteria, selection. *See* Selection criteria

Customers:
    as investors, 3(table), 42
    business plan and, 96-97, 99
    compared to consumers, 99
    ignorance in, 40, 47-50, 51-53, 54
    novelty to, 47-50, 51-53, 55
    primary and secondary, 99
    questions on, 133
    risk reduction and, 51-53
    strategic alliances with, 34-35
    value added to, 42-43

DCF. *See* Discounted cash flow analysis
Deadlock breakers, 153
Deal:
    in the business plan, 85(table), 112
    in the presentation, 121(table),
        126-127
    in the Q&A session, 134
    negotiation process for, 148-153
Debt:
    convertible, 137
    versus equity, 2, 108, 137, 151, 156
Declining balance depreciation, 145
Defensible position, 98, 99
Demand curve, 143-144
Depreciation, 145
Development financing, 3(table)
Disagreement, and negotiation, 149. *See
    also* Conflict
Discount rate, 110, 126, 138-140
Discounted cash flow (DCF) analysis, 138
Dispute resolution, 32. *See also* Conflict
Distinctive competence, 85(table), 91-94
Distribution of equity. *See* Equity
    allocation
Distribution systems, 101, 104
Dividend policy, 110
Due diligence:
    by boards of directors, 63
    by entrepreneurs, 8-9, 26
    by investors, 8, 11

Earnings before interest and taxes
    (EBIT), 111
EcoClear Inc., 13, 85-86, 88
Ego considerations, 71

Emotional factors, 5, 71
Employees:
    business plan and, 106
    cost assumptions and, 144-145
    financing from, 3(table)
    incentive contracts with, 34
    principal-agent problem and, 62-63
Emu Now, 65
Equity allocation:
    checklist for, 159(table)
    conflicts in, 20-27, 32
    dilution of, 28-29, 107
    in the business plan, 107, 112
    negotiation of, 148-153
    options on, 152-153
    ownership plan for, 28-32, 34, 37
    reasons for, 20
    recommendations on, 27-36
    roles and, 20-27, 157-158
    sequential, 31-32, 37
    to business planner, 23-24
    to inventor, 22-23
    to investors, 26-27, 140, 146-153
    to management, 24-26, 61, 63, 152-153
    valuing the business and, 140, 146-153
    *See also* Hurt money
Equity financing gap, 10
Equity versus debt, 2, 108, 137, 151, 156
eToys, 57
Evaluation:
    checklists for, 160(table), 161(table)
    of the business, 40-55, 158-159
    of the business plan, 82
    of the management team, 57-69,
        159-160
    *See also* Valuing the business
Executive summary, 84(table), 85-88,
    162-163
Expensing versus capitalization, 145

Failures, reasons for, 57-58, 65
Family, financing from, 3(table), 156
FIFO (first-in-first-out) method, 145
Financial call protocol, 32-33, 37
Financial details:
    in the business plan, 108-112
    in the presentation, 121(table),
        125-126

in the Q&A session, 134
Financial expertise, 60, 65, 66, 68
Financial statements, 111-112
Financial summary, 85(table)
Financing:
    creative, 150-153
    importance of, 1-2
    in stages, 137, 150
Financing, early-stage:
    amount of, 66
    categories of, 3(table)
    checklist for, 157(table)
    debt versus equity for, 2, 156
    sources of, 3(table), 4-15, 156-157
    sources of, largest, 9
    sources of, most common, 4
    timing for, 14, 66
First-in-first-out (FIFO) method, 145
First-stage financing, 3(table). *See also*
    Financing, early-stage
Follow-up markets, 46, 55, 102, 104
Follow-up products, 46, 54-55, 102, 104,
    124
Forums, venture capital, 8
Friends:
    financing from, 3(table), 156
    of the company, 64, 68
Funding, early-stage. *See* Financing,
    early-stage
Future value, 154(n2). *See also* Net
    present value
FutureBall, 49-50

Government bond rate, 143
Growth strategy, 102-103

Häagen-Dazs, 44
Harvest. *See* Time horizon
Human resources development plan, 125
Hurdle rate, 141, 143
Hurt money, 58, 62, 63, 68

iCat.Corp, 1, 2
idealab!, 57
Ignorance:
    in customers, 40, 47-50, 51-53, 54

in investors, 41, 54
in management, 40, 55, 64-68
in producers, 40, 50-51, 53-54
Imitation strategy, 43-44
Incentive structure:
    for management, 25, 34, 151-152, 153,
        159
    for other stakeholders, 34-35
    principal-agent problem and, 62-63
Income statement, 111
Incremental allocation, 31-32, 37
Industry analysis, 95
Inflation rate, premium on, 139
Information:
    communication strategy for, 73-74, 114
    lack of, as risk, 40-41
    novelty and, 48-49, 52-54
    *See also* Ignorance
Initial public offerings (IPOs), 6
Innovation, 1, 42, 45
Insurance, 66, 67
Intangible assets, 2
Intellectual property, 19, 22, 53
    investors' view of, 44-46
    ownership plan and, 28, 30
    questions on, 132
    web of protection for, 45
Interest rate, components of, 139
Internal rate of return (IRR):
    analysis of, 141-142, 143, 146
    in the business plan, 111, 112
    in the presentation, 126, 127
International studies, 10, 11
Inventor:
    awards for, 13
    equity allocation to, 22-23
    personality fit with, 25-26
    role of, 20, 22-23
Inventories, 145
Investment multiples, 142-143, 147
Investors:
    criteria for selecting, 9, 33-34, 42,
        149-150, 157
    criteria used by, 7, 41
    domain of, 41-42, 54
    equity allocation to, 26-27, 140,
        146-153
    evaluation from perspective of, 40-69
    exploitation by, 26, 38

how many to approach, 7, 140
how to approach, 8, 12-13
ignorance in, 41, 54
involvement by, 6-7, 11, 12, 35-36, 38,
    150
personality fit with, 26
preference of. *See* Preferences of
    investors
principal-agent problem and, 63
readiness of, 155
roles of, 20, 26-27, 35-36, 150, 151
scoring checklist for, 41
strategic alliances with, 71-73
time horizon for, 109-110, 127, 140,
    142-143, 146
valuing of, 27, 149-150
what they are looking for, 40-47,
    57-64, 158-160
Involvement:
    agreements on, 35-36, 38
    by business angels, 11, 12
    by venture capitalists, 6-7
    negotiation and, 150
    *See also* Roles
IPOs. *See* Initial public offerings
IRR. *See* Internal rate of return


Just-in-time (JIT) inventory
    management, 145


KFC, 45
Knowledge Adventure, 57


Laser Artistry Inc., 4
Laser Force, 4
Last-in-first-out (LIFO) method, 145
Leadership, of the CEO, 59, 68, 129, 130
Legal structure, 29, 36-37, 107
Letters of intent, 47
Liability of newness, 47-54, 55, 64-68, 158
Licensing, 53, 67
LIFO. See Last-in-first-out method
Limited liability partnership, 36-37
Logos, 45, 52, 114
Long-felt need, 44, 54

Management team:
    commitment of, 58, 62, 68
    complementarity of, 58-61, 68, 107,
        125
    distinctive competence of, 91
    equity allocation to, 24-26, 61, 63,
        152-153
    evaluation of, 57-69, 159-160
    experience of, 58, 61-62, 64-68,
        124-125
    hiring of, 25
    ignorance in, 40-41, 64-68
    incentive contracts with, 25, 34,
        151-152, 153, 159
    investment by, 58, 62, 63, 68, 159
    novelty to, 51, 64-68
    personality fit with, 25-26
    presentation of, 120(table), 124-125
    principal-agent problem and, 62-63
    quality of, 58-64, 107, 124-125
    resumes of, 112
    roles of, 19, 24-26, 59-60
    skills of, 19, 58-61, 68
    valuing of, 25
Manufacturers, novelty to, 50-51, 53-54
Manufacturing:
    cost of, 106, 144
    in the business plan, 85(table), 105-106
    risk reduction and, 53-54, 67
Marginal revenue, 143-144
Mark-up pricing rule, 144
Market environment, 85(table), 94-98,
    133
Market forces, and bargaining, 35
Market positioning, 85(table), 98-103,
    133
Market research, 47, 143
    business plan and, 96, 112
    questions on, 133
Market segments, 95-96
Market share, 102, 103
Marketing agreements, 52
Marketing expertise, 59-60, 68
Marketing mix, 100-102, 124
Marketing strategy, 98-103, 133
Markets, follow-up, 46, 55, 102, 104
Matchmaking services, 13-14
"Me too" strategy, 43-44
Memoranda of association, 29, 30

Microsoft Corporation, 122, 123
Mission statement, 89-90
MIT Business Angel Network, 14
Monopoly supplier of funds, 26, 140
MOOT CORP competition, 13
Multimedia, 121-124. *See also* Visual aids
Multiples, investment, 142-143, 147

Negotiation, 163-164
  keeping options open in, 8, 140
  process of, 148-153
Net present value (NPV):
  analysis of, 138-140
  analysis of, and IRR, 141, 146
  analysis of, and pricing, 144
  discount rate and, 138-140
  in the business plan, 87, 111, 112
  in the presentation, 126
Net profit after taxes (NPAT), 87, 111
Networks:
  of business angels, 12-13, 14
  of venture capitalists, 7
Newness, liability of, 47-54, 55, 64-68, 158
Nonvoting stock, 151
Novelty:
  liability of, 47-54, 55, 64-68, 158
  risk reduction and, 50, 51-54, 67-68
NPAT. *See* Net profit after taxes
NPV. *See* Net present value

Oceanic Products, examples:
  for communication strategy, 72
  for the business plan, 90-91, 93-94, 99-102, 105, 108, 110
  for the presentation, 123
ODR. *See* Opportunity discount rate
Offer. *See* Ask and offer
Operating expenses, 144
Operations, 85(table), 105-106, 125
Opportunity discount rate (ODR), 138-139, 141
Options, on equity allocation, 152-153
Organizational structure, 106-107
Outsourcing, 60. *See also* Consultants; Contracting
Overhead slides, 122-124

Ownership plan, 28-32, 34, 37, 158
Ownership structure, 107. *See also* Equity allocation; Legal structure

P/E ratio. *See* Price/earnings ratio
Page budget, 84-85(table), 162
Partnerships, 30, 36-37
Patents, 19, 45, 46, 55, 70, 114
Performance contracts, 34-35, 151-152, 153
Personal financing sources, 3(table), 4-5, 18
Personality fit, 25-26
Positioning, 98-103
PowerPoint, 122, 123
Preferences of investors, 6, 7, 12, 157
  in evaluating the business, 40-55
  in evaluating the managers, 57-69
Presentation:
  bullet points for, 122, 124
  checklist for, 164(table)
  content of, 115, 118-119, 120-127
  demeanor during, 117
  dress for, 116-117
  length of, 76-77, 119, 120-121(table)
  logical flow in, 77
  multimedia for, 121-124
  outline of, 120(table)
  plan for, 118-120
  purpose of, 74-75, 78-79, 160-161, 163
  sections of, 118, 163
  software for, 122, 123, 124
  strategic omissions/inclusions in, 75-76, 118-119, 135
  team members for, 116-118, 119
  time budget for, 118, 120-121(table)
  visual aids in, 78
PriCap, 14
Price/earnings (P/E) ratio, 140, 146-148
Price, selling:
  novelty and, 48
  superior value and, 42-43
  valuing the business and, 143, 144
Prima Facie Inc., 49, 64
Primary customers, 99
Principal-agent problem, 58, 62-63, 68
Private Capital Clearinghouse, Inc., 14
Proactive risk reduction, 109(table), 125

Producers:
  ignorance in, 40, 50-51, 53-54
  novelty to, 50-51, 53-54, 55
  risk reduction and, 53-54

Products:
  follow-up, 46, 54-55, 102, 104, 124
  in the business plan, 85(table), 90-91
  in the presentation, 120(table)

# About the Authors

**Dean A. Shepherd** is Assistant Professor in Entrepreneurship and Strategy at the Lally School of Management and Technology, Rensselaer Polytechnic Institute and was 1997 Visiting Scholar in Entrepreneurship at the J.L. Kellogg Graduate School of Management, Northwestern University. His research has resulted in papers to be published in the *Journal of Business Venturing* and the *Journal of Small Business Management* as well as papers published in the *Academy of Management Best Papers Proceedings*. He also has published another book in the Sage Series on Entrepreneurship and the Management of Enterprises, namely, *New Venture Strategy; Timing, Environmental Uncertainty and Performance*. He has presented papers at Frontiers of Entrepreneurship Research conferences, Academy of Management meetings, and the 1997 ICSB meeting, where his paper won best theory paper of the conference.

Dr. Shepherd received his doctorate and MBA from Bond University (Australia) and a Bachelor of Applied Science from the Royal Melbourne Institute of Technology. He was a member of the Bond team that placed second in the MOOT CORP competition in 1993, and in the following years he assisted the Bond University team as co-academic advisor. These teams placed first in 1994, second in 1995, and first in 1996. He has established two family businesses and has taken an equity stake and advisory role in the footwear technology venture that emanated from the 1994 MOOT CORP team. Dr. Shepherd's research interests include new venture strategy, venture capital, and the decision making of entrepreneurs. His teaching fields include entrepreneurship, strategy, and management.

**Evan J. Douglas** is Professor and Head of the Graduate School of Business at Queensland University of Technology, Brisbane, Australia. His teaching and research interests include entrepreneurship, new venture planning, new venture funding, international business, competitive strategy, strategic pricing, quality and warranty decisions, and managerial economics. His publications include two university textbooks and a variety of papers on applied microeconomic issues. He has owned and operated small businesses in Canada and in the United States, and currently is director and/or has equity in several start-up companies. His Bachelor and Master of Commerce degrees are from the University of Newcastle, Australia, and his PhD is from Simon Fraser University, Canada. He has won excellence-in-teaching awards in his 25 years of experience in business education at eight universities in Australia, Canada, and the United States. In the past 4 years, he has acted as academic advisor to MBA teams that have finished first, twice and second, twice in the annual International MOOT CORP Entrepreneurship competition.